# Kids' Party Cookbook!

## by
## Penny Warner

**Meadowbrook Press**

Distributed by Simon & Schuster

New York

Library of Congress Cataloging-in-Publication Data

Warner, Penny.
    Kids' party cookbook! / by Penny Warner.
          p. cm.
       Includes index.
       ISBN 0-88166-279-8 (pbk. : Meadowbrook). — ISBN 0-671-57373-X
    (pbk. : Simon & Schuster)
       1. Cookery.   2. Entertaining.   3. Children's parties.   I. Title.
    TX731.W36   1996
    641.5—dc20                                                   96-28401
                                                                 CIP

ISBN 0-88166-279-8

Simon & Schuster Ordering # 0-671-57373-X

Copyright © 1996 by Penny Warner

Editor: Liya Lev Oertel

Proofreader: Ranae Lammle

Production Manager: Amy Unger

Graphic Designer: Linda Norton

Text Illustrations: Laurel Aeillo

Cover Illustration: Gwen Connelly

Published by Meadowbrook Press, 18318 Minnetonka Boulevard, Deephaven, MN 55391.

BOOK TRADE DISTRIBUTION by Simon & Schuster, a division of Simon and Schuster, Inc., 1230 Avenue of the Americas, New York, NY 10020.

00 99 98 97 96    6 5 4 3 2 1

Printed in the United States of America.

# DEDICATION

To Tom, Matthew, and Rebecca,
The icing on my cake.

# ACKNOWLEDGEMENTS

Thanks to the following party chefs, tasters, and revelers, who helped make this the perfect party cookbook: Charles Anderson, Dave Cabral, Craig Clemetson, Jason Cosetti, Tara Cuebel, Jonathan Ellington, Steven Ellington, Brian Hurley, Geoffrey Pike, Jim Russell, Brie Saunders, Darci Sutton, Jana Swec, Joe Swec, Tim Swec, Sue Stadelhofer, Mia Thiele, Heather Thornton, Samuel Valdez, Zachary Valdez, Jennifer Ware, Alex Warner, Nick Warner, and Dakota Webster.

A special thanks to Bruce Lansky, Liya Lev Oertel, and Joel Mondshane at Meadowbrook Press.

# TABLE OF CONTENTS

# INTRODUCTION

Successful parties require only a few ingredients: friends, fun, favors, and FOOD! For many kids, the best part of any party is the food: snacks, treats, and drinks made festive for the event. After all the excitement of playing games, doing activities, and opening presents, the young guests are always ready to refuel with refreshments.

*Kids' Party Cookbook* provides you with recipes for fun and festive party treats that are healthier than the traditional high-sugar, high-junk-food goodies. Don't worry, you won't have to substitute bran and tofu for cake and ice cream. Believe it or not, it is possible to serve your guests something that tastes good and is good for them—and this book shows you how!

The recipes in *Kids' Party Cookbook* are creative, unique, fun to eat, and easy to make, with healthy alternatives for every recipe. The easy-to-follow recipes include a list of ingredients and materials needed, directions for preparing the food, variations on the recipe, and practical tips. You'll also find information on the number of servings, the time it takes to prepare the recipes, and the level of complexity of each recipe.

When planning a party menu, check out the recipes in the *Kids' Party Cookbook*, choose what you like, and then serve the Creative Cakes and Ice-Cream Dreams along with some Snappy Snacks, Dazzling Drinks, Mini-Meals, and Dynamite Desserts. When the party's over, send the guests home with a handful of Fun Food Favors.

This helpful and fun book also contains ten chapters that offer ideas for fun-to-eat holiday foods, from New Year's Eve Treats to Christmas Cheer, all to help you celebrate the festivities with family and food. There are Valentine's Day Sweets for your sweetheart, St. Patrick's Celebrations for the Irish in you, Easter Edibles for friends of the rabbit, Purim and Passover Parties for traditional Jewish holidays, Fourth of July Favorites for America's birthday, Halloween Hungries for hungry little monsters, Thanksgiving Goodies for family gatherings, and Hanukkah Huzzah for the celebration of lights.

Remember, while we want the kids to be happy and enjoy the celebration, we want them to be healthy too. An occasional indulgence in a slightly decadent treat is fine, but if we can make the treat nutritious too, we're sure to please everyone. So, for fast, easy, healthy fun, just follow the recipes in the *Kids' Party Cookbook*!

# SERVING TIPS AND SUGGESTIONS

## WHAT TO SERVE

Whether you're serving cake and ice cream, snacks and treats, or creative mini-meals, be sure to offer healthy treats as well as the traditional party goodies to balance the intake of sweets. At the beginning of the party, set out bowls of nuts, trail mix, fruit, or cheese and crackers for nibblers to help themselves. Or select something from the Snappy Snacks chapter, such as Rainbow Wands or Pick 'n' Chewsies. All you need is a little imagination to turn simple and healthy servings into festive foods.

Before serving dessert, line your guests' tummies with the four food groups with Shish-Ka-Snack, Painted Sandwiches, or any other small meal from the Mini-Meals chapter. To help wash down the snacks and treats, pour healthy fruit drinks that are colorful, festive, and nutritious, such as a Banana Blitz or a Strawberry Sizzle.

For dessert, serve such yummy yet healthy treats as the Fancy Flower Cake or the Johnny Appleseed Cake from the Creative Cakes chapter. Also, follow the recipes from the Ice-Cream Dreams chapter, which includes such soon-to-be favorites as Cherry Chill and Chocolate Noodles (which call for low-fat or nonfat frozen yogurt or sorbets instead of high-fat ice cream). Or turn to the Dynamite Desserts chapter and offer your guests such alternatives to cake and ice cream as Nut Cracker Pie or Banana Peanut Butter Cheesecake.

As the festivities come to an end, send your guests home with fun-to-eat food favors that double as healthy snacks, such as Edible Jewelry or Secret Stash Chipmunk Chow.

## WHEN TO SERVE

Offer the kids a light snack when they arrive to keep them from getting tired, cranky, and hungry. Don't overfeed them before the party games or they'll be too full to participate. After the kids burn up some of their energy playing the party games and doing the activities, gather them on the lawn or at the table for your party refreshments. After cake and ice cream, allow some time for the food to settle while opening presents. Then send them out the door with a bag of treats from the Fun Food Favors chapter, in case they get hungry on the way home!

## HOW MUCH TO SERVE

Younger party guests have small appetites, so keep the serving sizes small and cut up all the refreshments into bite-sized pieces. Then let them eat as much or as little as they want. Older kids however usually know what and how much they want to eat, so just let them help themselves.

When serving the cake and ice cream, offer small slices and scoops. The kids will be fairly full from the previous snacks and meals, and many will probably not finish their desserts. Tell them that they can always ask for more if they finish the first round. And always have plenty of food—you don't want to run out!

## SERVING A BALANCE OF FOODS

Try to keep the four food groups in mind when planning the snacks and meals. You can supply the dairy products by adding low-fat milk to the shakes. For the fruit and veggie group, offer bite-sized fruit snacks or veggie dips. Small bags of mixed cereals or creative sandwiches will cover the wheat and grain group. And cheese with crackers, peanut butter, or chopped nuts will add to the protein group. Even cake can cover all four food groups, if you serve a carrot cake with a peanut butter milkshake!

## SPECIAL CONSIDERATIONS

**Age and Number of Guests:** There are several guidelines regarding the number of guests. Some experts suggest inviting one guest for every year of the child's age. For example, if the child is four years old, invite four friends. Others say to invite the number you can manage and get help for larger groups. Some kids like to have the whole class over, while others prefer only one or two close friends, so you'll have to negotiate the numbers.

When you invite relatives and family members, the number of guests will depend on the size of your family. Just remember, children tend to be over-stimulated during a celebration, and smaller groups can help keep the party atmosphere a little more manageable and pleasant.

**Allergies:** Check with all the parents of your invited guests to see which children might have food allergies (allergies are common in early childhood). If you're offering cake and ice cream and a child is allergic to wheat, milk, or sugar, try to create an alternative that's just as fun and tasty to eat so that child doesn't feel odd or left out.

**Picky Eaters:** Don't force the guests to eat anything they don't want, but encourage them to give each treat a taste. Then ask for their evaluations. Offer the picky eater an alternative if possible, but don't cater to every child's whim. If they don't like what's served and you've tried alternatives, they will survive.

## SERVING SUGGESTIONS

**Fun Ways to Present Food:** Be creative in your presentation and you'll find the guests are more apt to eat what you serve. Cut the sandwiches into interesting shapes and let the kids build their meals with the parts. Add eyes, a mouth, and a nose with raisins, chocolate chips, sprinkles, and so on to liven up the foods. Shape the hotcakes into hearts, the cheese slices into alphabet letters, or the pretzels into people. Make ice-cream-cone clowns to serve with a giant clown cake.

**Fun Ways to Serve Food:** To make the party food special, serve it up on decorative plates, with matching cups and napkins and a handful of plastic silverware, all coordinated with your party theme. You can also look for fun, unbreakable containers, such as large seashells, colorful tins, fancy plates and glasses, wicker baskets, nesting toys, pet dishes, plastic margarine bowls, juice cans, party boxes, funny mugs, muffin tins, lunch boxes, decorated bags, empty clean toys, and so on. You might serve the snacks in carved out fruit or vegetables, such as a pumpkin shell for a bowl or an orange shell for an ice-cream dessert. Or serve hobo lunches by wrapping the food in bandannas that you hang on sticks. In addition, you may want to personalize each place with pictures, artwork, games, puzzles, and favors. With a little extra effort, the food will be an event in itself!

**Fun Names to Give Foods:** Kids are much more likely to try a new food when it has a funny name. All it takes is a little imagination. You can get ideas from the names of a favorite animal, character, or superhero, or just think up silly names, using words that kids love, such as Hot Lava, Quicksand, Mooseberry Juice, or Squeezers. Who can resist a Hamburger Cookie, Sarsaparilla Soda, Jurassic Hatch, Tuna Quackers, Mystery Cupcakes, Avalanche!, Sand 'n' Ants, or Dirt 'n' Worms? Yummy!

**Other Enticements:** Play games at the table while you eat the refreshments to make the meal-time even more fun! You can incorporate the food into a party game—the cake can serve as the table centerpiece, or it can be part of the party fun. For example, let each guest decorate his or her own slice of cake or cupcake with tubes of cream cheese frosting, and then add granola, candy sprinkles, little flowers, tiny toys, miniature marshmallows, chocolate or carob chips, sugar-free lollipops, chopped nuts, low-sugar cereals, or paper cutouts. Or just let the kids eat while they play word games, paper and pencil games, or whatever they like.

# DO-IT-YOURSELF VERSUS GETTING HELP

You can do it all yourself if you have the time and energy. If you plan the details in advance and make a checklist to review each day, you'll be prepared by the party date.

The food is easy—you can freeze some of it, or have the guests help you make it during the party as an activity. If you feel you need help with the food preparation or any part of the party, call the parents of the guests and ask them to join you, or hire neighborhood teenagers to help you out both ahead of time and on the party day. If you need help, get it. You want to enjoy the party too!

# TRICKS FOR ADAPTING OLD FAVORITES FOR 90s KIDS

If the kids have favorite foods they can't give up but you don't feel they are as nutritious as they could be, sneak in good nutrition and the guests will never know the difference. You can add oat bran to the cake batter or wheat germ to the muffin mix, cut down on sugar without the kids noticing, switch from butter to margarine or low-fat spread, mix your recipes with nonfat milk instead of whole, tint whole-wheat bread instead of white for sandwiches, and so on. You should always look for creative ways to give good nutrition without sacrificing good taste. Serve juice drinks instead of sodas; angel food or carrot cake instead of high-sugar, high-fat cake; and nonfat yogurt or sorbets instead of regular ice cream. There are millions of ways to add good nutrition to old favorites!

And now, it's *Kids' Party Cookbook* time!

# Party Recipes

# SNAPPY SNACKS

Your energetic party guests will need some super snacks to tide them over until the cake and ice cream arrive. Keep the treats handy—in serving bowls placed around the party room or on the table—so that everybody can help themselves. Snacks help give energy, so your guests can stay active, alert, and involved in the party fun. And they help prevent the guests from getting cranky before the party ends.

The following recipes offer a wide variety of easy-to-make and easy-to-serve Snappy Snacks that provide a healthy alternative to the high-fat chips and high-sugar cookies you so often see at parties. And you can make most of them as a party activity.

# AQUARIUM JELL-O

You never know what you'll find under the sea with Aquarium Jell-O. Make these mini-aquariums and fill them up with funny fish!

- **Serves:** 6
- **Time:** 15 minutes to prepare
  2 hours to set
- **Complexity:** Easy

## INGREDIENTS

- 1 package blue- or green-tinted sugar-free Jell-O
- 1 cup boiling water
- 1 cup cold water
- 24 Gummy Fish
- 1 cup low-fat, low-sugar whipped cream
- Fish crackers (optional)

## MATERIALS

- 6 clear plastic cups

## WHAT TO DO

**1** Make blue or green Jell-O according to package directions.

**2** When Jell-O is slightly cooled, divide it among 6 plastic cups.

**3** Add 3 (or more) Gummy Fish to each cup.

**4** Place cups in refrigerator for 2 hours, until Jell-O is firm.

**5** At serving time, top with whipped cream to form "surf."

**6** Serve with fish crackers (optional).

**VARIATIONS:** Make the Jell-O and pour it into one large bowl shaped like an aquarium or a fish bowl. Allow to cool a few minutes; then add Gummy Fish. When the Jell-O sets, serve from the fish bowl. Or pour the Jell-O into muffin tins sprayed with vegetable spray. When the Jell-O sets, turn out onto a big platter for your guests to enjoy.

**PRACTICAL TIP:** Allow the Jell-O to cool and set a short time before adding the Gummy Fish, so they don't sink to the bottom.

# BANANA BUNS

Hot dog buns make great snack servers. You can fill them up with all kinds of creative treats. For a foot-long, fun-to-eat food, try our Banana Buns. Served with a glass of milk, they make a complete meal.

- **Serves:** 4
- **Time:** 10 minutes to prepare
  30 to 45 seconds to heat in microwave or
  5 minutes to heat in oven
- **Complexity:** Easy

## INGREDIENTS

- 4 bananas, peeled
- 4 whole-wheat or low-fat hot dog buns
- ½ cup low-fat, low-sugar peanut butter
- Raisins (optional)
- Low-fat coconut, shredded (optional)
- Peanuts, chopped (optional)

## MATERIALS

- Microwave or oven
- Microwavable plates (for microwave) or aluminum foil (for oven)
- Knife for spreading

## WHAT TO DO

**1** Place peeled banana in hot dog bun.

**2** Spread peanut butter on both halves of the bun.

**3** Top with raisins, coconut, and chopped peanuts. (This step is optional.)

**4** Heat in microwave for 30 to 45 seconds, or wrap in foil and heat in oven at 350 degrees for 5 minutes, until warmed.

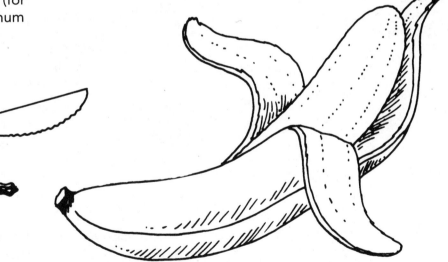

**VARIATION:** For a sweeter taste, spread low-sugar jelly on one side of hot dog bun and peanut butter on the other.

**PRACTICAL TIP:** Microwave the Banana Buns one at a time. Do not microwave too long or the buns will become tough and chewy.

# BIG BITE

Everybody loves cookies—and the bigger, the better. For an extraspecial dessert, instead of cake, make a giant cookie!

- **Serves:** 8 to 10
- **Time:** 20 minutes to prepare 15 to 25 minutes to bake (depending on cookie recipe instructions)
- **Complexity:** Easy

## INGREDIENTS

- Favorite chocolate chip, oatmeal raisin, or peanut butter cookie recipe (or see page 208 and 209 for our recipes)
- Tubes of frosting in a variety of colors, with decorator tips
- Vegetable spray

## MATERIALS

- Piece of heavy cardboard the size of a large pizza, covered with aluminum foil, or large plastic tray
- Cookie sheet, round or rectangular
- Toothpick

## WHAT TO DO

**1** Prepare cookie dough according to recipe directions.

**2** On cookie sheet sprayed with vegetable spray, shape the entire ball of cookie dough into a large circle, square, triangle, heart, or other shape, about ½-inch thick.

**3** Bake 5 to 10 minutes longer than the recipe requires to be sure the cookie is done in the middle. Test with a toothpick.

**4** When the cookie is cool, carefully slide it onto foil-covered cardboard or plastic tray.

**5** Decorate the cookie, using tubes of frosting and tips: make a border around the edge of the cookie, create simple designs and shapes, and/or write the birthday child's name in the center.

**6** Display the Big Bite cookie for all to see. Then break off little bites for the guests to enjoy.

**VARIATIONS:** Do steps 1 through 4 before the guests arrive, and then have them help decorate the cooled cookie as one of the party activities. Use a variety of frosting colors to make the cookie more festive.

**PRACTICAL TIPS:** If you make your own cookie recipe, use only half the recommended sugar and substitute whole-wheat flour for half the white flour. If you buy ready-made frosting, make sure it's low-fat or fat-free. If you make the cookie the day before, wrap it in foil to keep it moist.

# BURGER BABIES

These Burger Babies are the cutest cookie sandwiches you'll ever see. And your guests will love to make them as well as eat them!

- **Serves:** 10
- **Time:** 20 to 30 minutes to prepare
- **Complexity:** Easy

## INGREDIENTS

- 20 low-salt, low-sugar vanilla wafers
- 10 round chocolate-covered mints, sugar-free if desired
- 1 cup low-fat coconut
- Food coloring, green
- Poppy or sesame seeds

## MATERIALS

- 10 paper plates
- Plastic bag, medium-sized
- Microwave

## WHAT TO DO

**1** Give each guest a paper plate, 2 vanilla wafers, and 1 chocolate mint.

**2** Have the guests place the mint on top of one wafer.

**3** Place coconut in the plastic bag, add several drops of food coloring, and shake the bag until coconut is tinted green.

**4** Have the guests sprinkle coconut over chocolate mint and place second wafer on top to make a hamburger sandwich.

**5** Heat in microwave for 10 seconds to melt the chocolate mint slightly. Press lightly to secure.

**6** Place a drop of water on top of Burger Baby, and then top with a sprinkle of poppy or sesame seeds. Serve.

**VARIATIONS:** To add more color, squirt a small amount of red frosting onto half of the chocolate mint to make catsup, and yellow frosting on the other half of the mint to make mustard. If you really want to be decadent, use a chocolate-covered Oreo cookie between the vanilla wafers and secure with frosting.

**PRACTICAL TIP:** Tint the coconut before the guests arrive so it has a chance to dry; otherwise the green food coloring may come off on the fingers.

# CLONE COOKIES

The guests can make miniatures of themselves with these creative Clone Cookies

- **Serves:** 12
- **Time:** 15 minutes to prepare dough
  8 to 10 minutes to bake
  20 minutes to prepare clones
- **Complexity:** Easy

## INGREDIENTS

- 1 package gingerbread mix or favorite gingerbread recipe, using half the sugar (or see page 210 for our recipe)
- ⅓ cup whole-wheat flour
- Decorative candies, such as red hots, sprinkles, chocolate chips, raisins, and so on
- Tubes of frosting and decorator tips
- 1 quart nonfat frozen vanilla yogurt

## MATERIALS

- Rolling pin
- Cookie cutter in shape of gingerbread figure
- Cookie sheet
- 12 paper plates

## WHAT TO DO

**1** Make gingerbread, following package directions or using recipe, but add a little extra whole-wheat flour to make the dough stiffer.

**2** Preheat oven to 350 degrees.

**3** Roll the dough out to ⅛-inch thickness.

**4** Cut out figures with cookie cutter, 2 for each guest; place on cookie sheet; and bake at 350 degrees for 8 to 10 minutes. Cool.

**5** Pass out one cookie on a paper plate to each guest; and set aside the other cookies.

**6** Let each guest decorate the cookie in his or her own image, using the candy decorations and tubes of frosting.

**7** Spread softened frozen yogurt on plain cookies. Top with decorated cookies, pressing gently to fill in spaces.

**8** Eat immediately!

**VARIATIONS:** Slice frozen yogurt into 1-inch-thick pieces and cut out gingerbread figures with cookie cutter. Refreeze until time to assemble the cookies. Use different flavors of frozen yogurt for variety.

**PRACTICAL TIP:** After the guests are finished decorating, freeze the Clone Cookies for a while to avoid melt-down and drips.

# COOKIE CANVAS

Give your guests paintbrushes and a variety of edible "paints," and let them turn their treats into works of art.

- **Serves:** 8 to 10
- **Time:** 15 minutes to chill
  20 to 30 minutes to prepare
  8 to 10 minutes to bake
- **Complexity:** Easy

## INGREDIENTS

- Favorite sugar cookie recipe, using half the required sugar (or see page 209 for our recipe)
- Food coloring in a variety of colors
- 1 egg, separated

## MATERIALS

- Small paintbrushes for all the guests
- Aluminum foil
- Small bowls for food coloring
- Cookie cutters
- Cookie sheet

## WHAT TO DO

1 Make the sugar cookie dough and chill it in the refrigerator for 15 minutes.

2 Gather the guests at the table and divide the dough among them.

3 Let the guests flatten dough and cut it into shapes with cookie cutters or make their own shapes.

4 Mix several drops of food coloring with a little egg yolk in individual bowls. Set the bowls in the center of the table.

5 Have the guests paint their cookies, using the paint brushes and the food coloring mixture.

6 Glaze the cookies with egg white mixed with a little water.

7 Transfer the cookies to a cookie sheet, and bake at 350 degrees for 8 to 10 minutes. Eat your art!

**VARIATIONS:** Divide the dough into four large balls and tint each ball with a different food coloring. Divide the colored dough among the kids so each guest gets four colors. Then let them create faces, animals, monsters, and so on, using the colored dough.

**PRACTICAL TIPS:** Have the guests work on small pieces of foil to prevent the cookies from sticking to the work surface and to make it easy to transfer them to the cookie sheet. Start preheating the oven about 15 minutes before the guests finish decorating.

# COOKIE POPS

You can find practically anything on a stick, so why not a cookie? And your guests will love this fun way to serve party snacks!

- **Serves:** 10
- **Time:** 20 minutes to prepare
  10 minutes to chill
- **Complexity:** Easy

## INGREDIENTS
- 20 sugar-free vanilla wafers or other single-layer cookie
- ½ cup low-fat, low-sugar peanut butter
- 1 6-ounce bag carob, chocolate, or white chocolate chips
- Candy sprinkles or tubes of frosting (optional)

## MATERIALS
- Knife
- 10 ice-cream sticks
- Wax paper
- Microwave or stove
- Microwave-safe dish or double boiler

## WHAT TO DO

**1** Spread peanut butter over flat side of the cookies.

**2** Press an ice-cream stick into the peanut butter on half the cookies.

**3** Top with another cookie so the stick is sandwiched between the two cookies.

**4** Melt chips in microwave or over a double boiler, stirring until smooth.

**5** Dip cookie pops in the melted chips, covering completely.

**6** Set the cookie pops on wax paper, stick side up, and sprinkle with candy sprinkles before the coating sets.

**7** Place in refrigerator to chill.

**8** Make funny faces or designs with tubes of frosting, if desired, and serve.

**VARIATIONS:** If using white chocolate chips, tint the melted chocolate with food coloring. To make Flower Pops, spread cookies with peanut butter. Then set "petals" cut from fruit leather around outside edge, add ice-cream sticks, and top with a second cookie to secure stick and petals.

**PRACTICAL TIPS:** Allow the excess coating to drip into pan before setting the cookie on the wax paper. Work quickly to cover the coating with sprinkles before the coating sets.

# CREEPY CRAWLY CATERPILLARS

Here's a way kids can eat all the caterpillars they want—with their parents' approval! These Creepy Crawly Caterpillars tingle and tickle the tummy.

- **Serves:** 6
- **Time:** 15 minutes to prepare
- **Complexity:** Easy

## INGREDIENTS
- 3 large bananas
- 12 stick pretzels
- 2 containers low-fat banana, lemon, or other fruit yogurt
- Unsweetened coconut or granola (optional)

## MATERIALS
- Knife
- 6 small plates

## WHAT TO DO

1 Slice bananas into ¼-inch rounds and divide among 6 plates, placing the edge of one banana round on top of another, making a curved line of overlapping banana slices.

2 Stick 2 pretzels into the top banana round in a V-shape to make antennae.

3 Spread yogurt over the top of all the slices.

4 Sprinkle on coconut or granola, if desired.

5 Add legs with small pretzel bits, if desired.

**VARIATION:** You can turn the banana rounds up on their ends and connect them with pretzel sticks.

**PRACTICAL TIP:** These are fun for the kids to make, so let them help. Just provide them with their own plates to work on, and have everything counted out before beginning.

# FALSE TEETH

**T**hese funny False Teeth will get your guests giggling in no time—they will love to make them and eat them!

- **Serves:** 8
- **Time:** 15 minutes to prepare
- **Complexity:** Easy

## INGREDIENTS

- 2 red apples
- ½ cup low-fat, low-sugar peanut butter or low-fat cream cheese or low-fat spreadable cheese
- 32 cubes low-fat cheese, cut the size of miniature marshmallows
- 8 dried apricot slices
- 1 cup shredded low-fat cheese

## MATERIALS

- Knife
- 8 small paper plates

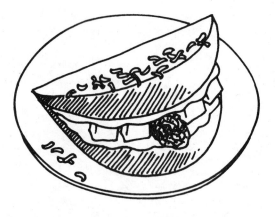

## WHAT TO DO

**1** Slice 1 apple into eighths to make 8 wedges. Repeat for other apple.

**2** Spread peanut butter, cream cheese, or spreadable cheese on one side of each wedge.

**3** Place 4 cheese cubes on the spread to make teeth.

**4** Top with a second wedge to form mouth.

**5** Add apricot slice sticking out to form tongue.

**6** Sprinkle shredded cheese on top to make mustache.

**7** Smile and eat.

**VARIATIONS:** To make Raspberry Mouths, omit the cheese "teeth" and simply stick the apricot "tongue" out from between the two apple "lips." To make Goofy Eyeballs, spread peanut butter or spreadable cheese on apple wedges and lay them open, forming a circle; place a grape in the center to form an eyeball; and add shredded cheese for lashes.

**PRACTICAL TIP:** Let the guests make these snacks on small plates so the False Teeth don't have to be moved when they are finished.

# Flutter-Byes

Let the guests help you make these crunchy cuties, or make them yourself and surprise your guests!

- **Serves:** 8
- **Time:** 20 minutes to prepare
- **Complexity:** Easy

## Ingredients

- 4 stalks of celery
- 1 cup low-sugar, low-fat peanut butter; low-fat cream cheese; or low-fat spreadable cheese
- 16 large twist-type pretzels, plus a few extras
- 32 raisins

## Materials

- Spoon (for filling the celery)
- 8 small plates

## What To Do

**1** Clean celery stalks and cut into 4-inch pieces.

**2** Fill celery pieces with peanut butter, cream cheese, or spreadable cheese.

**3** Place a pretzel on either side of celery to form butterfly wings.

**4** Use extra pretzel pieces to make antennae.

**5** Add raisins to make eyes or body decorations.

**VARIATIONS:** Tint the cream cheese and make the Flutter-Byes in different colors. Or let the guests create their own flying insects, using the ingredients.

**PRACTICAL TIP:** Have the guests work on plates so they don't have to move the Flutter-Byes when they're finished.

# LEAPIN' LIZARD

It looks frightening, but this exciting snack isn't likely to scare your guests. It will only make them laugh.

- **Serves:** 8
- **Time:** 15 minutes to prepare
  30 minutes to cool
- **Complexity:** Easy

## INGREDIENTS

- ½ cup low-fat, low-sugar peanut butter
- 1 12-ounce package marshmallows
- 4 to 6 drops food coloring, green
- 4 cups Rice Krispies, Cheerios, Corn Flakes, or other low-sugar cereal
- Raisins
- Vegetable spray

## MATERIALS

- Large pan
- Rectangular pan
- Knife
- Wax paper

## WHAT TO DO

**1** Heat peanut butter and marshmallows in large pan; stir until smooth.

**2** Add green food coloring and mix well.

**3** Pour in cereal, stir quickly, and pour contents into rectangular pan sprayed with vegetable spray.

**4** Cool in refrigerator. When cool, cut into 4 long strips, lengthwise.

**5** Set 3 of the strips in the shape of a large Z along the center of the table on a sheet of wax paper.

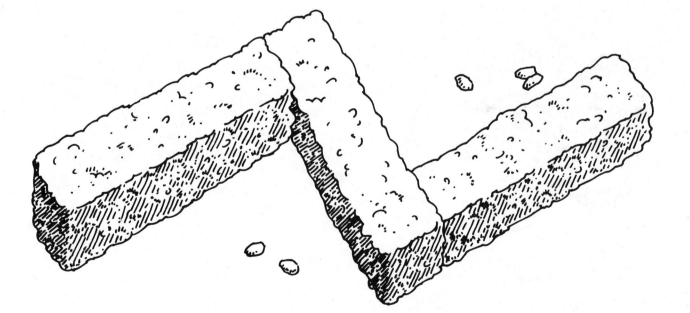

# Snappy Snacks

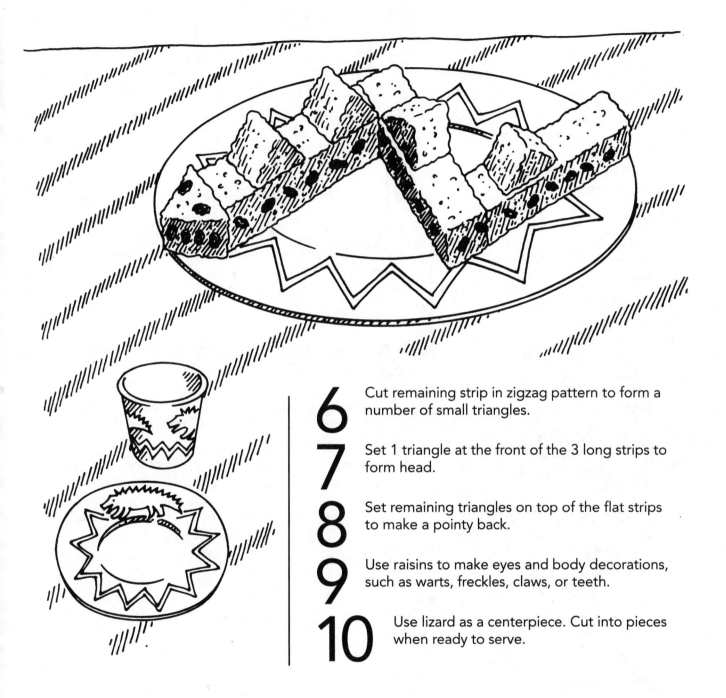

**6** Cut remaining strip in zigzag pattern to form a number of small triangles.

**7** Set 1 triangle at the front of the 3 long strips to form head.

**8** Set remaining triangles on top of the flat strips to make a pointy back.

**9** Use raisins to make eyes and body decorations, such as warts, freckles, claws, or teeth.

**10** Use lizard as a centerpiece. Cut into pieces when ready to serve.

**VARIATIONS:** With a little creative cutting, you can make a dinosaur, snake, caterpillar, or anything you like. Just color the mixture to suit.

**PRACTICAL TIP:** Be generous with the vegetable spray so you can easily remove the mixture from the pan.

# MINI-MICE

The kids can make their own fun-to-eat Mini-Mice as part of the party activity. And with a little creativity, you can morph the mice into whatever you want!

- **Serves:** 5
- **Time:** 15 to 20 minutes to prepare
  8 to 10 minutes to bake
- **Complexity:** Easy

## INGREDIENTS

- 1 10-ounce package of refrigerator biscuit dough
- ¼ cup sesame, poppy, or sunflower seeds
- Raisins
- 5 shoelace-thin licorice whips

## MATERIALS

- Aluminum foil
- Cookie sheet

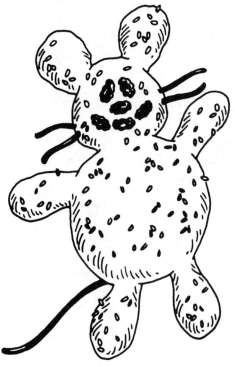

## WHAT TO DO

**1** Preheat oven to 400 degrees.

**2** Separate biscuits into 10 individual servings and give the kids 2 biscuits each, along with a sheet of foil to work on.

**3** Divide biscuit into 2 parts to form head and body of mouse.

**4** Divide second biscuit into 6 pieces to form ears, hands, and feet.

**5** Roll larger sections of dough into balls. Then set on cookie sheet, head on top of body. Flatten slightly.

**6** Round the smaller pieces and press them where the ears, hands, and feet should be. Sprinkle with seeds to make fur, and press raisins into dough for eyes, nose, and mouth.

**7** Transfer the Mini-Mice to a cookie sheet, and bake at 400 degrees for 8 to 10 minutes, until golden brown.

**8** When the Mini-Mice are cool, add licorice whips for whiskers and tail.

**VARIATIONS:** Let the kids make the dough into any animal shape they want: cats, bears, turtles, ladybugs, dinosaurs, or monsters. Tint the dough and make it colorful, and decorate the animals' faces with tubes of frosting for added fun.

**PRACTICAL TIP:** Don't let the mice get too thick or too thin or they won't bake properly.

# FROGGY FACE

These happy Froggy Face snacks bring a goofy grin to all your party guests.

- **Serves:** 4
- **Time:** 20 minutes to prepare
  2 hours to set in refrigerator
- **Complexity:** Easy

## INGREDIENTS

- 1 3-ounce package sugar-free lime gelatin
- 1 cup boiling water
- 1 8-ounce carton plain or lime nonfat yogurt
- 1 cantaloupe
- 8 strawberries
- 8 raisins

## MATERIALS

- Large bowl
- Mixer
- Knife (to cut the melon)
- Paper towel or napkin
- Large spoon
- 8 toothpicks

## WHAT TO DO

**1** In a large bowl dissolve gelatin in boiling water. Stir in yogurt.

**2** Chill mixture until thick but not set. Then beat at highest speed until nearly doubled in volume.

**3** Cut melon in half, scoop out seeds, and pat dry with paper towel.

**4** Scoop whipped mixture into centers of melon. Chill until firm.

**5** Cut melons in half again, lengthwise, so you have 4 large slices.

**6** Remove stems from strawberries and insert raisins into stem hole.

**7** Stick toothpicks into 2 strawberries (one toothpick for each strawberry), sideways, and insert them on top of melon slice to form frog's eyeballs, with raisin pupils showing.

**8** Smile at your grinning Froggy Face. Then eat!

**VARIATIONS:** Use a variety of gelatin flavors to create your own smiling creatures. Substitute grapes for the strawberries, or use them for noses.

**PRACTICAL TIPS:** Make sure the gelatin mixture is firm before slicing the melon in half in step 5, so it keeps its shape. Serve immediately.

# PICK 'N' CHEWSIES

Let the guests pick 'n' choose whatever they want from a variety of fixings. The more you can add to the picks, the more fun for the choosers!

- **Serves:** 8 to 10
- **Time:** 15 minutes to prepare
  15 minutes to serve and eat
- **Complexity:** Easy

## INGREDIENTS

- ½ to 1 cup each: raisins, dried fruit, banana chips, grapes, cherries, peanuts, walnuts, almonds, pecans, pretzels, low-fat corn chips, small crackers, sesame seeds, sunflower seeds, granola, unsweetened cereals, toasted oats, toasted coconut, low-sugar cookie crumbs, carob chips, and so on

## MATERIALS

- Medium bowls, 1 for each ingredient
- Small bowls or bags, 1 for each guest
- Small plastic spoons for ingredient bowls and guests

## WHAT TO DO

1. Pour the small, healthy snack items into separate bowls.

2. Place the bowls around the table, along with a serving spoon for each.

3. Give each guest a small bowl, decorative party bag, or small plastic bag.

4. Have the guests walk around the table and pick and choose whatever they like, spooning the munchies into their bowls or bags.

5. Eat with fingers, spoons, chopsticks, or other fun kitchen utensil.

**VARIATIONS:** Provide a variety of fruits and vegetables and let the guests make their own salads. Or make a taco bar, breakfast bar, sundae bar, or anything bar!

**PRACTICAL TIPS:** Tell the guests to take only 1 spoonful per bowl so there will be plenty for everyone. If anything is left over, have the guests go around the table a second time and take a refill.

# PREHISTORIC BUGS

Let the kids discover the wonders of archeology—prehistoric bugs captured in amber!

- **Serves:** 4 to 6
- **Time:** 15 minutes to prepare
  2 hours to chill
- **Complexity:** Easy

## INGREDIENTS

- 1 tablespoon packaged gelatin
- ¼ cup water
- 1½ cups apple juice
- ¼ cup apple juice concentrate
- Raisins, miniature chocolate chips, chocolate sprinkles, or other tiny candies

## MATERIALS

- Medium bowl
- Medium pot
- Individual clear cups or bowls for each guest
- Small magnifying glasses for each guest (optional)

## WHAT TO DO

**1** Mix together gelatin and water in a bowl. Let stand 1 minute.

**2** Pour apple juice and concentrate into a pot and bring to a boil.

**3** Add hot juice to gelatin mixture and stir until dissolved.

**4** Pour mixture into individual clear cups or bowls.

**5** Sprinkle with a few raisins, chocolate chips, chocolate sprinkles, or other tiny candies.

**6** Place in refrigerator and chill until firm.

**7** Serve with magnifying glasses for fun.

**VARIATION:** Pour the mixture into a large pan instead of individual cups, and place in refrigerator. When the mixture is firm, cut into squares and give each guest a section to examine for Prehistoric Bugs.

**PRACTICAL TIP:** If serving in individual containers, use clear cups or bowls so the guests can see the bugs easily.

# RAINBOW WANDS

These colorful snacks on a stick are almost too beautiful to eat. But your guests will manage anyway!

- **Serves:** 6
- **Time:** 20 minutes to prepare
- **Complexity:** Easy

## INGREDIENTS

- Red fruit, such as watermelon balls, strawberries, or cherries
- Orange fruit, such as orange sections, cantaloupe balls, mango, or papaya
- Yellow fruit, such as pineapple cubes or banana slices
- Green fruit, such as green grapes, honeydew melon balls, or kiwi slices
- Blue fruit, such as large blueberries
- Purple fruit, such as purple grapes or cut-up plums

## MATERIALS

- Knife
- 6 wooden skewers
- Medium bowls, 1 for each fruit

## WHAT TO DO

**1** Clean and cut fruit into bite-sized pieces that can be assembled on a skewer.

**2** Place fruit in separate bowls, and line the bowls up according to colors of the rainbow: red, orange, yellow, green, blue, purple.

**3** Give each guest a skewer and have them assemble their Rainbow Wands.

**VARIATIONS:** Make Caterpillars instead of Rainbow Wands by using the same fruits, but having the guests assemble them onto a stick pretzel. Just have them push the pretzel into the fruit as they would a toothpick. Let them use chocolate sprinkles for eyes on their Caterpillars. Or assemble the Rainbow Wands yourself and present them as a surprise to the guests at snack time. Add other items, such as tinted marshmallows, tinted bread cubes, colored vegetables, and so on, to the skewers.

**PRACTICAL TIP:** After the guests have skewered the fruit, break off the sharp tips to prevent accidental injury.

# ROCKY-ROW BOATS

Pop these peel-and-eat Rocky-Row Boats right out of the oven and let the kids sail them down their hungry tummies.

- **Serves:** 4
- **Time:** 10 minutes to prepare
  5 minutes to bake
- **Complexity:** Easy

## INGREDIENTS

- 4 bananas
- ½ cup raisins, carob chips, or chocolate chips
- ½ cup low-sugar miniature marshmallows
- ½ cup nuts, chopped

## MATERIALS

- Spoon
- Medium bowl
- 8 ice cream sticks
- Aluminum foil
- 4 medium plates

## WHAT TO DO

**1** Preheat oven to 350 degrees.

**2** Peel back the curved-in section of banana, but don't remove peeling.

**3** Carefully scoop out banana, cut it into small chunks, and place the chunks into a bowl.

**4** Add raisins or chocolate chips, marshmallows, and chopped nuts. Stir well.

**5** Fill each banana shells with the same amount of mixture, and replace opened peel.

**6** Wrap each banana in foil, and heat in oven for 5 minutes, until warm and soft.

**7** Remove banana from oven, peel back loose strip, and stick two ice-cream stick "oars" into the sides.

**8** Serve to the guests on individual plates. Let the guests use the "oars" to eat from the "canoe," or offer them spoons.

**VARIATIONS:** Add peanut butter to the mixture instead of marshmallows for a healthier alternative. Add other fruits to the mixture too, such as apple chunks, pineapple bites, grapes, and so on.

**PRACTICAL TIPS:** If the guests help, have them handle the bananas carefully so they don't fall apart. Place a sheet of foil under their work areas so they can simply wrap it around the bananas after stuffing them. Have them open the foil and bananas carefully since they're hot.

# Slime Monsters

**W**anna get slimed? Make up a batch of these colorful Slime Monsters and serve them to your Ghostbusters.

- **Serves:** 12
- **Time:** 20 minutes to prepare
  30 minutes to freeze
- **Complexity:** Easy

## Ingredients

- 1 12-ounce package white chocolate chips
- 3 tablespoons vegetable oil
- Food coloring, green
- 6 bananas
- Tubes of frosting in a variety of colors

## Materials

- Microwave or stove
- Microwavable bowl or double boiler
- Spoon
- Knife

## What To Do

**1** Pour the white chocolate chips and oil into a microwavable bowl or double boiler. Heat until the chips are melted.

**2** Add several drops of green food coloring. Stir until mixture is smooth.

**3** Slice unpeeled bananas in half, crosswise; carefully slice around the banana peel at the halfway point; and peel off top half, leaving the bottom half intact.

**4** Dip the peeled ends of the bananas into the chocolate mixture, covering the peeled half and about ¼ inch of the unpeeled half.

**5** Turn peeled side up, and allow the green slime to harden a few minutes.

**6** Decorate a funny face on the chocolate with tubes of frosting.

**7** Place the bananas in the freezer for 30 minutes or more. Remove and serve.

**Variations:** You can use regular chocolate chips to make Gorilla Guys; or tint the white chocolate other colors besides green, to make Pink Phantoms, Big Yellow Birds, or Blue Ghosts. Use whole bananas to make giant-sized monsters. Instead of decorating the monsters before they are frozen, freeze them first; then let the guests decorate the funny faces themselves.

**Practical Tips:** The bananas don't have to be frozen, but they hold up better if they are. Place melted white chocolate in a small, deep container, for easier dipping.

# SNAP, CRACKLE, AND EAT!

The buffet bar gives your guests a chance to make their own snacks, which they're much more likely to eat and enjoy. Just be sure to have plenty of choices so everyone gets a bite of something they love for their original cereal-and-toppings combination!

- **Serves:** 8
- **Time:** 10 minutes to prepare 20 minutes to serve and eat
- **Complexity:** Easy

## INGREDIENTS

- 8 bowls of 8 different low-sugar cereals, about 1 cup each
- 8 bowls of toppings, such as strawberries, blueberries, cantaloupe balls or chunks, raisins, banana slices, dried fruit, coconut, chopped almonds, about 1 cup each
- Low-fat or nonfat whipped cream
- 8 maraschino cherries
- Low-fat or nonfat milk

## MATERIALS

- 8 small bowls
- Serving spoons, 1 for each bowl of cereal and each bowl of fruit
- 8 small spoons

## WHAT TO DO

**1** Place bowls of cereals and toppings, whipped cream, and milk on a table or on tables around the room.

**2** Give each guest a small bowl and let them begin at the cereal station, collecting whatever cereals they want in their bowls.

**3** Have the guests move to the toppings and add a second layer to the cereal.

**4** Have them add a squirt of whipped cream, some milk, and a cherry on top!

**VARIATIONS:** Tint the whipping cream or the milk pink, blue, or yellow to add a splash of color.

**PRACTICAL TIP:** Remind the kids to take only 1 or 2 spoonfuls of each item so there will be enough for everyone.

# TWISTERS

Your guests can create their own personalized pretzels and shape them any way they want—into monsters, designs, or even their names!

- **Serves:** 4
- **Time:** 10 minutes to prepare
  15 minutes for yeast to rise
  10 minutes to bake
- **Complexity:** Easy to Medium

## INGREDIENTS

- 2 tablespoons yeast
- 1 cup warm water
- 1 tablespoon honey
- 2⅔ cups flour (part whole-wheat, if desired)
- 1 teaspoon salt
- 2 eggs, beaten
- Mustard, catsup, or melted cheese dip

## MATERIALS

- Large bowl
- Aluminum foil
- Cookie sheet

## WHAT TO DO

**1** In a large bowl dissolve yeast in warm water. Let sit for 15 minutes

**2** Add honey, flour, and salt. Knead until smooth.

**3** Let dough rise for 10 to 15 minutes in a warm spot.

**4** Preheat oven to 425 degrees.

**5** Divide dough into fourths and distribute a fourth to each guest. Have them roll and shape the dough into snakes, faces, or alphabet letters.

**6** Place dough shapes on foil-lined cookie sheet, and brush with beaten eggs. Bake at 425 degrees for 10 minutes.

**7** Serve with mustard, catsup, or melted cheese dip.

**VARIATIONS:** Tint the dough different colors to give your Twisters a little more pizzazz. Sprinkle poppy seeds, sesame seeds, or mild spices over the Twisters to enhance the flavor.

**PRACTICAL TIPS:** Have the guests roll the dough out on individual sheets of foil so it's easy to transfer the Twisters to a cookie sheet. For puffier pretzels, let the dough rise twice, before and after you shape it.

# DAZZLING DRINKS

Your guests will get thirsty while eating all that great food and playing games. So be sure to have plenty of drinks on hand to quench those dry throats.

We've whipped up a great collection of thirst quenchers for kids. These Dazzling Drinks offer a variety of healthy ingredients, along with a refreshing taste. Feel free to add your own creativity when concocting these super sippers. When creating your own drinks, keep good nutrition in mind. You can substitute fruit juice for soda, and make it bubbly with a little sugar-free carbonated water. Or use nonfat frozen yogurt instead of ice cream to make your blender shakes. And add milk whenever you can.

To prevent broken glass, serve the party drinks in plastic glasses. Most supermarkets carry a variety of plastic glasses in different shapes and colors. I especially recommend using plastic champagne glasses—the real ones are breakable and expensive to replace.

Now try the following recipes for some refreshing, tasty, and healthy party drinks!

# APPLE JAZZ

This smooth, fruity drink is a great thirst quencher, and all the ingredients are healthy.

- **Serves:** 4
- **Time:** 5 minutes to prepare
- **Complexity:** Easy

## INGREDIENTS
- 1 16-ounce jar applesauce
- 1 12-ounce can frozen orange juice concentrate mixed with three cans of water

## MATERIALS
- Blender
- 4 glasses

## WHAT TO DO

**1** Pour half the applesauce and orange juice into blender.

**2** Whirl until smooth.

**3** Repeat steps 1 and 2 with remaining ingredients.

**4** Serve.

**VARIATION:** Substitute apple juice concentrate for orange juice concentrate for a rich, appley taste.

**PRACTICAL TIP:** Serve in hollow oranges for fun.

# APPLE-NUT FLOAT

This nutty, fruity float combines kids' favorite treats and covers three food groups!

- **Serves:** 4
- **Time:** 5 minutes to prepare
- **Complexity:** Easy

## INGREDIENTS

- 1 cup milk
- 1 cup nonfat frozen vanilla yogurt
- 1 cup low-sugar applesauce
- 2 tablespoons smooth peanut butter
- 2 ice cubes

## MATERIALS

- Blender
- 4 glasses

## WHAT TO DO

**1** Combine half of each ingredient in blender.

**2** Whirl until smooth.

**3** Repeat steps 1 and 2 with remaining ingredients.

**4** Pour into glasses and serve.

**VARIATION:** Top with a scoop of flavored nonfat frozen yogurt.

**PRACTICAL TIP:** Crush ice cubes first for easier preparation.

# BANANA BLITZ

A Banana Blitz should relieve that party thirst with its milky, fruity, smooth taste. And it's high in fiber and good nutrition!

- **Serves:** 4
- **Time:** 5 minutes to prepare
- **Complexity:** Easy

## INGREDIENTS

- 3 cups fresh (or frozen in low sugar) strawberries
- 3 bananas
- 3 cups nonfat milk
- 1 tablespoon vanilla
- 8 to 10 ice cubes

## MATERIALS

- Blender
- Clear fancy glasses
- Straws

## WHAT TO DO

**1** Prepare strawberries and bananas.

**2** Place half of each ingredient in blender.

**3** Whirl until smooth and fluffy.

**4** Repeat steps 2 and 3 with remaining ingredients.

**5** Serve with straws in clear glasses.

**VARIATIONS:** Instead of strawberries, use other fruits, such as cantaloupe, pineapple, or other berries. To make a shake, substitute nonfat vanilla yogurt for milk.

**PRACTICAL TIP:** For easier blending, chop up strawberries and bananas and break up ice cubes (or use ice chips).

# BANANA-BUTTER GUZZLER

Peanut butter and bananas in a frosty shake? Your guests will love this crazy concoction—and they won't even know how good this guzzler is for them!

- **Serves:** 4
- **Time:** 5 minutes to prepare
- **Complexity:** Easy

## INGREDIENTS
- 2 ripe bananas
- 3 cups nonfat frozen yogurt
- ½ cup smooth, low-fat, low-sugar peanut butter

## MATERIALS
- Knife
- Blender
- 4 glasses

## WHAT TO DO

**1** Cut bananas into pieces.

**2** Place half of each ingredient in blender.

**3** Whirl until smooth.

**4** Repeat steps 2 and 3 with remaining ingredients.

**5** Pour into glasses and serve.

**VARIATION:** To make a drink instead of a shake, use nonfat milk.

**PRACTICAL TIP:** Dividing ingredients in half prevents overflow.

# BEETLE JUICE

What are a few bugs in the punch when those bugs are full of good nutrition? Hee-hee!

- **Serves:** 6
- **Time:** 5 minutes to prepare
  2 hours to set ice
- **Complexity:** Easy

## INGREDIENTS

- Raisins
- 1 16-ounce bottle cranberry juice cocktail
- 1 12-ounce can lemonade concentrate, thawed

## MATERIALS

- Ice cube tray
- Large pitcher
- 6 clear glasses

## WHAT TO DO

**1** Several hours before the party, prepare ice cubes by pouring water into ice cube tray and adding 3 or 4 raisins to each section to make "beetles."

**2** Freeze until firm.

**3** At serving time, pour cranberry juice cocktail, lemonade concentrate, and 4 cans of water into the pitcher. Stir.

**4** Pour Beetle Juice into glasses and serve with one or two beetle ice cubes.

**VARIATIONS:** Mix the lemonade concentrate with lemon-lime soda for a carbonated, bubbly drink. Add more raisins to the ice cubes to make the drink crawling with beetles.

**PRACTICAL TIP:** Serve in clear glasses so the kids can see the Beetle Juice clearly.

# CELEBRATION BUBBLY

To make the party even perkier, serve this delightful drink that tickles the tummy. Offer your Celebration Bubbly to the kids in grown-up glasses to make it extraspecial.

- **Serves:** 8
- **Time:** 5 minutes to prepare
- **Complexity:** Easy

## INGREDIENTS

- 1 32-ounce can low-sugar apple or cranberry juice
- 1 16-ounce bottle sugar-free 7-Up or bubble water
- 8 strawberries or other cut-up fruit (optional)

## MATERIALS

- Large pitcher
- Long spoon (for mixing)
- 8 plastic champagne, wine, brandy, or other fancy glasses

## WHAT TO DO

**1** Mix together apple (or cranberry) juice and 7-Up (or bubble water) in a large pitcher.

**2** Pour into fancy plastic glasses.

**3** Drop a strawberry (or other fruit) into the glass for a special effect.

**VARIATION:** Substitute strawberry nectar for apple juice for "pink champagne."

**PRACTICAL TIPS:** You can buy plastic champagne glasses at party supply stores. Freeze the cherries or strawberries before serving them in the drinks for an icy addition. Pour the bubbly in front of the guests—during pouring, the fizz and bubbles are at maximum strength.

# CHOCOBERRY SHAKE

An unusual combination that even the adults will like, so make extra for the helping hands.

- **Serves:** 4
- **Time:** 5 minutes to prepare
- **Complexity:** Easy

## Ingredients
- 1 pint fresh (or frozen in low sugar) strawberries
- 1 banana
- ¼ cup sugar-free chocolate syrup
- 2 cups nonfat milk

## Materials
- Knife
- Blender
- 4 glasses

## What To Do

1 Clean and slice berries.

2 Slice banana.

3 Combine half of each ingredient in blender.

4 Whirl until smooth.

5 Repeat steps 3 and 4 with remaining ingredients.

6 Pour into glasses and serve with strawberry and banana garnish (optional).

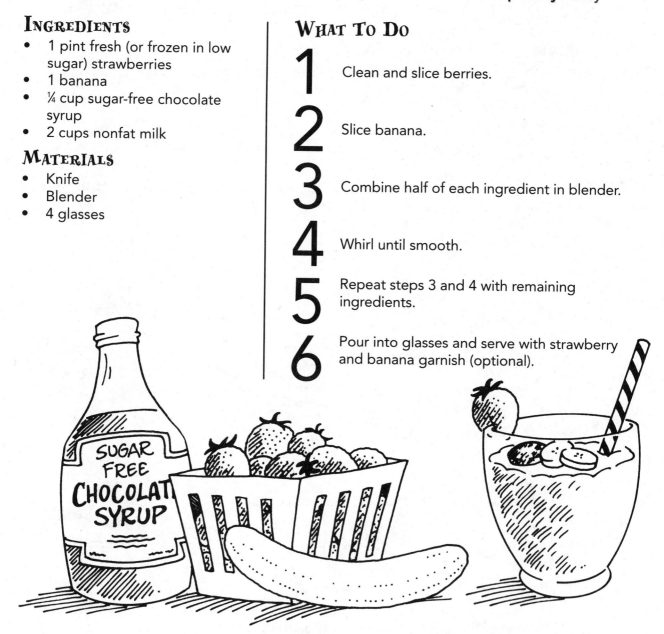

**Variations:** Instead of strawberries, use other fresh or frozen berries, such as raspberries, boysenberries, or blueberries.

**Practical Tip:** You may want to whirl the fruit in the blender before adding liquid to get it chopped up for easier blending.

# CHOCOLATE SPARKLE

Here's a fun way to make a chocolate drink sizzle! Your guests will love the tickly taste!

- **Serves:** 4 to 5
- **Time:** 5 minutes to prepare
- **Complexity:** Easy

## INGREDIENTS

- 2 cups sugar-free 7-Up
- 2 cups nonfat milk
- 4 tablespoons sugar-free chocolate syrup

## MATERIALS

- Blender
- Fancy glasses, 1 for each guest
- Crazy straws (optional)

## WHAT TO DO

**1** Combine half of each ingredient in blender.

**2** Whirl on high until well blended and frothy.

**3** Repeat steps 1 and 2 with remaining ingredients.

**4** Serve in fancy glasses with crazy straws for fun.

**VARIATIONS:** Use strawberry syrup or vanilla extract, or offer the kids a choice of chocolate, vanilla, or strawberry.

**PRACTICAL TIP:** You can make this drink without a blender, but it's more fun to drink when it's frothy.

# COOKIE DUNKER

Why serve the milk and cookies separately when you can combine the two favorites and make a Cookie Dunker drink!

- **Serves:** 4
- **Time:** 5 minutes to prepare
- **Complexity:** Easy

## INGREDIENTS

- 2 cups nonfat milk
- 1 pint nonfat frozen vanilla yogurt
- 4 low-sugar, low-fat cookies, such as black-and-white sandwich cookies, mint sandwich cookies, peanut butter cookies, or graham crackers, crushed

## MATERIALS

- Blender
- 4 glasses

## WHAT TO DO

1 Combine 1 cup nonfat milk with 1 cup frozen yogurt and 2 crushed cookies in blender.

2 Whirl until smooth and well blended.

3 Repeat steps 1 and 2 with remaining ingredients.

4 Pour Dunker into glasses, and serve with a matching whole cookie.

**VARIATIONS:** Try other frozen yogurt flavors. Use chocolate milk instead of regular milk.

**PRACTICAL TIP:** For a smoother drink, crush the cookies well before placing in blender.

# Juicy Milk

Quick, easy, colorful, and nutritious!

- **Serves:** 4     • **Time:** 5 minutes prepare     • **Complexity:** Easy

## Ingredients
- 3 cups nonfat milk
- 1 cup sugar-free grape juice
- 2 bananas

## Materials
- Blender
- 4 clear glasses

## What To Do

**1**   Place half of each ingredient in blender.

**2**   Whirl until smooth.

**3**   Repeat steps 1 and 2 with remaining ingredients.

**4**   Pour into glasses.

**Variation:** Substitute other fruit juices or drinks for the grape juice.

**Practical Tip:** Chop up the bananas for easier blending.

# MOKKA-CHINO

Serve the kids a hot cocoa drink that tastes like a mocha cappuccino. Don't forget to use coffee mugs for this special treat!

- **Serves:** 4
- **Time:** 10 minutes to prepare
- **Complexity:** Easy

## INGREDIENTS

- 4 teaspoons cocoa powder
- 4 tablespoons honey
- 4 cups low-fat milk
- 4 teaspoons instant decaffeinated coffee mix

## MATERIALS

- Spoon (for stirring)
- Saucepan
- 4 coffee mugs

## WHAT TO DO

**1** Place cocoa, honey, and 1 cup of milk into saucepan. Stir until blended.

**2** Gradually pour in remaining milk.

**3** Heat over low flame until warm, stirring frequently.

**4** Add coffee granules and mix well.

**5** Serve in coffee mugs.

**VARIATIONS:**  Omit the coffee and add mint or vanilla.

**PRACTICAL TIPS:** You can heat this drink in the microwave. Be sure to mix the milk in slowly so it blends well.

# MONKEY MILKSHAKE

This drink may not keep them swinging from the trees, but it will satisfy even a tropical thirst.

- **Serves:** 4
- **Time:** 5 minutes to prepare
- **Complexity:** Easy

## INGREDIENTS

- 4 cups nonfat milk
- 2 medium bananas
- 2 teaspoons unsweetened cocoa

## MATERIALS

- Blender
- 4 coconuts (optional) or 4 glasses
- 4 straws

## WHAT TO DO

**1** Combine half of each ingredient in blender.

**2** Whirl until smooth.

**3** Repeat steps 1 and 2 with remaining ingredients.

**4** Pour into hollow coconut shells or glasses and serve with straws.

**VARIATION:** Pour coconut milk into the blender with the rest of the ingredients.

**PRACTICAL TIP:** Break bananas into chunks for easier blending.

# ORANGE-U-THIRSTY?

Here's a quick and nutritious cool-down if you are having a hot time at the party. This drink is versatile, too, and can be adapted to other fruit flavors, so choose your favorite!

- **Serves:** 6 to 8
- **Time:** 5 minutes prepare
- **Complexity:** Easy

## INGREDIENTS

- 1 12-ounce can frozen orange juice concentrate
- 3 cups nonfat milk
- 1 pint low-fat orange sherbet or frozen orange yogurt

## MATERIALS

- Blender
- 6 to 8 cups or glasses (the smaller the container, the more guests you can serve)
- Spoons and wide straws, 1 for each guest

## WHAT TO DO

**1** Place half of each ingredient in blender.

**2** Whirl until smooth.

**3** Repeat steps 1 and 2 with remaining ingredients.

**4** Pour into cups or glasses, and serve with a wide straw and a spoon.

**VARIATIONS:** Try a variety of fruit drinks and frozen yogurts for creative new tastes.

**PRACTICAL TIP:** Add some ice cubes to the blender to make the drink ice cold and frosty.

# PEPPERMINT POWERHOUSE

If your guests like peppermint, they will love this refreshing drink with a bubbly tingle. It looks like a peppermint candy and tastes like one too!

- **Serves:** 4
- **Time:** 5 minutes prepare
- **Complexity:** Easy

## INGREDIENTS

- 2 cups low-sugar apple juice
- 1 pint nonfat strawberry sorbet or frozen yogurt
- ⅛ teaspoon peppermint extract
- 1 12-ounce bottle bubble water

## MATERIALS

- Large pitcher
- Spoon
- 4 glasses

## WHAT TO DO

**1** Combine apple juice, 1 cup sorbet or frozen yogurt, extract, and water in large pitcher.

**2** Mix until sorbet is melted and blended.

**3** Pour into glasses and add 1 scoop (¼ cup) sorbet to each glass.

**VARIATION:** Let the guests stir their drinks with peppermint sticks for added fun.

**PRACTICAL TIPS:** Soften half the sorbet before mixing the beverage, for easier blending. Keep the other half frozen until serving time.

# PURPLE PEOPLE PLEASER

This Purple People Pleaser is sure to please all your guests, even if they aren't purple!

- **Serves:** 6
- **Time:** 5 minutes to prepare
- **Complexity:** Easy

## INGREDIENTS

- 1 16-ounce can fruit cocktail in juice
- 1 12-ounce can frozen grape juice concentrate mixed with three cans of water

## MATERIALS

- Blender
- 6 clear glasses

## WHAT TO DO

1  Combine half of each ingredient in blender.

2  Whirl until smooth.

3  Repeat steps 1 and 2 with remaining ingredients.

4  Serve in clear glasses.

**VARIATION:** Freeze the fruit cocktail in ice cube trays and serve with lemonade. Let the kids eat the fruit when they're finished with the drink.

**PRACTICAL TIP:** For easier blending, whirl fruit cocktail before adding liquid.

# RAINBOW FLOATS

Make multicolored milk with matching ice-cream floaters.

- **Serves:** 6
- **Time:** 10 minutes to prepare
  30 to 45 minutes to freeze
- **Complexity:** Easy

## INGREDIENTS

- 1 pint nonfat frozen vanilla yogurt
- 6 cups nonfat milk
- Food coloring: pink, orange, yellow, green, blue, and purple

## MATERIALS

- 6 bowls
- Spoon
- 6 glasses
- Straws and spoons, 1 for each guest

## WHAT TO DO

**1** Soften frozen yogurt for several minutes.

**2** Divide into 6 equal parts and place in individual bowls.

**3** Using food coloring, tint each of the 6 parts of yogurt a different color.

**4** Refreeze yogurt until firm.

**5** At serving time pour six glasses of milk.

**6** Using a few drops of food coloring, tint each glass of milk with one of the colors you used for the yogurt.

**7** Add a scoop of matching frozen yogurt to each glass of milk.

**8** Serve with a straw and a spoon.

**VARIATIONS:** Mix the colors of milk with different colors of yogurt for fun. Have the kids stir the two together and see what new color they get.

**PRACTICAL TIP:** After tinting, refreeze yogurt in small cups or in freezer forms.

# SUFFERIN' SARSAPARILLA SODA

As Sylvester the Cat would say, saddle up your sidekicks for a Sufferin' Sarsaparilla Soda, and watch the surprise as the drink turns pink and foamy.

- **Serves:** 6
- **Time:** 5 minutes to prepare
  2 hours to freeze
- **Complexity:** Easy

## INGREDIENTS
- 6 cherries
- 6 tablespoons grenadine syrup
- 6 12-ounce cans sugar-free cream soda

## MATERIALS
- Ice cube tray
- Spoon
- 6 glasses

## WHAT TO DO

**1** Place cherries into individual compartments of an ice cube tray, cover with water, and freeze (at least 2 hours before you will need them).

**2** Spoon 1 tablespoon of grenadine syrup into each glass.

**3** Drop an ice cube with frozen cherry inside into each glass.

**4** Pour cream soda into glasses while your guests watch.

**5** Serve.

**VARIATIONS:** Place a variety of small fruit bite, such as grapes, banana, kiwi, strawberries, and so on, in ice cube tray.

**PRACTICAL TIPS:** Make the cherry ice cubes the day before, so on the day of the party all you'll need to do is pop them into the glasses. This is a fun one to make in front of your guests, so let them watch or even help.

# SUNSHINE SQUEEZE

Capture the sunshine and serve it in these big, bright, yellow balls!

- **Serves:** 4
- **Time:** 15 minutes to prepare
- **Complexity:** Easy

## INGREDIENTS
- 4 grapefruit
- 1 cup lemonade
- 1 cup nonfat frozen lemon yogurt
- 1 cup sugar-free lemon-lime soda

## MATERIALS
- Blender
- Strainer
- 4 fancy straws

## WHAT TO DO

**1** Make a hole at the top of each grapefruit and hollow out insides.

**2** Strain juice and discard pulp.

**3** Combine the strained grapefruit juice, lemonade, frozen yogurt, and soda in blender.

**4** Whirl until smooth.

**5** Pour liquid into hollow grapefruit. Serve with a straw sticking out of the hole at the top.

**VARIATIONS:** Use orange shells instead of grapefruit to serve the drinks, and substitute orange juice for lemonade.

**PRACTICAL TIPS:** Use an apple corer to poke the hole into the grapefruit. Scrape out insides of grapefruit with melon baller or sharp-edged spoon.

# STRAWBERRY SIZZLE

Strawberries, strawberries, and more strawberries. Yum! And the bubbles in this strawberry extravaganza will make your guests giggle.

- **Serves:** 4
- **Time:** 5 minutes to prepare
- **Complexity:** Easy

## INGREDIENTS
- 2 cups frozen strawberries
- 1 cup low-fat milk
- 2 cans sugar-free strawberry soda
- 4 fresh strawberries

## MATERIALS
- Blender
- 4 tall glasses
- 4 straws

## WHAT TO DO

**1** Place frozen strawberries, milk, and soda in blender.

**2** Whirl until smooth.

**3** Divide drink among 4 glasses.

**4** Insert straw into each fresh strawberry and place straw-skewered strawberry in drink. Serve.

**VARIATIONS:** Use other fruits and fruit sodas for exciting new combinations. Other fruits that work well are cantaloupe, pineapple, or orange slices.

**PRACTICAL TIPS:** Blend half of the ingredients at a time—to prevent spillovers. Choose large fresh strawberries so the straws fit through them without breaking them.

# TROPICAL TORNADO

Whirl up a Tropical Tornado in the blender and turn a summer heat wave into a frosty blizzard in a glass!

- **Serves:** 6
- **Time:** 5 minutes to prepare
- **Complexity:** Easy

## INGREDIENTS

- 1 cup crushed pineapple in juice
- 1 ripened banana
- ½ cup coconut creme or piña colada mix
- 2 cups nonfat milk
- 1 pint nonfat frozen vanilla yogurt

## MATERIALS

- Blender
- Paper umbrellas (optional)
- 6 glasses

## WHAT TO DO

**1** Combine half of each ingredient in blender.

**2** Whirl until smooth.

**3** Repeat steps 1 and 2 with remaining ingredients.

**4** Pour into glasses and serve with paper umbrellas.

**Variations:** Substitute coconut or pineapple sherbet for yogurt for an additional punch.

**Practical Tip:** Serve the drinks in fancy plastic glasses for extra fun.

# MINI-MEALS

If the party will be a long one or if it takes place during mealtime, you might want to provide a small, nutritious meal before serving cake and ice cream. Try to design the meal to the party theme, and make the presentation creative and fun to eat. If you're hosting a pirate party, you might serve Surprise Inside or Spear-Fishing Dip. For a space party, offer the kids Twinkle Sandwiches or Shish-Ka-Snack. Or change the names of our mini-meals to fit the theme of your party.

The creative mini-meals that follow provide good nutrition along with fun.

# BIG RED FLOWER

These stuffed tomatoes look like giant red flowers ready to burst.

- **Serves:** 6          - **Time:** 20 minutes to prepare          - **Complexity:** Easy

## INGREDIENTS
- 6 large ripe tomatoes
- 6 cups store-bought or homemade potato salad

## MATERIALS
- Knife
- Spoon
- 6 small nonpoisonous flowers, real or artificial
- 6 plates

## WHAT TO DO

**1** Prepare tomatoes by slicing them in half almost to the bottom, leaving the bottom intact.

**2** Slice the tomato crosswise, leaving the bottom intact.

**3** Slice each quarter in half to make 8 wedges in tomato.

**4** Press wedges open gently, without separating the wedges completely.

**5** Fill the center of each tomato with potato salad.

**6** Press wedges up, to form flower.

**7** Top with a real or an artificial flower.

**8** Serve on individual plates.

**VARIATIONS:**     Fill the tomato with macaroni or pasta salad.

**PRACTICAL TIP:**  Remove some of the tomato pulp if you need more room for the potato salad.

# SHISH-KA-SNACK

Let the kids harpoon their own treats to create a Shish-Ka-Snack. You provide the skewers and snacks; the kids will provide the fun!

- **Serves:** 4
- **Time:** 10 minutes to prepare
  6 minutes to broil
- **Complexity:** Easy

## INGREDIENTS

- 1 banana, cut into 8 chunks
- 1 apple, cut into 8 chunks
- 8 chunks of pineapple
- ½ cantaloupe, cut into 8 cubes or balls
- 4 brown-and-serve low-fat turkey sausage links, cooked and cut into quarters
- 8 cubes low-fat baked ham (optional)
- 2 whole-wheat raisin English muffins, cut into bite-sized pieces, or 2 cinnamon raisin bagels, cut into bite-sized pieces
- 4 tablespoons low-fat margarine, melted

## MATERIALS

- Knife
- Medium bowls, 1 for each ingredient
- 4 skewers
- Broiler pan
- Broiler
- 4 plates

## WHAT TO DO

1 Prepare ingredients as described above and place in separate bowls.

2 Give each guest a skewer.

3 Let each guest skewer the fruit, meat, and bread from the bowls, as desired.

4 Place the filled skewers on a broiler pan and baste with melted margarine.

5 Place under broiler for 3 to 4 minutes, turn, and broil another 2 to 3 minutes until hot and sizzling.

6 Serve on individual plates.

**VARIATIONS:** Select any fruits, meats, or breads you like. Prepare the skewers ahead of time if you prefer.

**PRACTICAL TIPS:** Remind your guests that the food and the skewers are hot and tell them to remove the food carefully. Serve with milk for a complete meal.

# BURGER PIE

Turn an old family favorite into a new, fun party treat. You'll know that you are feeding your guests a nutritious meal, and they will have fun discovering the surprise inside this Burger Pie.

- **Serves:** 8
- **Time:** 15 minutes to prepare
  1 hour to cook
- **Complexity:** Easy

## INGREDIENTS

- 1 pound lean ground beef
- Ingredients for favorite meat loaf recipe
- 3 cups mashed potatoes, your favorite recipe or from a package
- 1 cup cheddar cheese, grated
- Catsup
- Mustard
- Pickles

## MATERIALS

- Cake pan
- Large plate
- 8 plates

## WHAT TO DO

**1** Make your favorite meat loaf recipe, and bake it in a cake pan instead of in a meat loaf pan, according to your recipe directions.

**2** Remove meat loaf from oven and turn it onto a plate.

**3** Make mashed potatoes.

**4** Cover entire meat loaf with mashed potatoes, as if frosting a cake.

**5** Sprinkle cheddar cheese around outside edge of meat loaf.

**6** Make a funny face on top using catsup, mustard, and pickles for mouth, nose, and eyes.

**7** Place on the table for all to admire. Then slice into servings and serve on individual plates.

**VARIATIONS:** Tint the mashed potatoes for fun. Instead of a face, make designs, or write the kids' names, using catsup and mustard squeeze bottles.

**PRACTICAL TIPS:** Drain off excess grease when meat loaf is done. To save time, make the mashed potatoes while the meat loaf is baking and keep them warm until needed to "frost" the meat loaf.

# CLOUD IN A CUP

An unusual variation on macaroni and cheese, a proven kids' favorite, this pretty, puffy Cloud in a Cup will delight your guests.

- **Serves:** 8
- **Time:** 20 minutes to prepare
  30 minutes to cook
- **Complexity:** Moderate

## INGREDIENTS

- 1 cup macaroni
- ½ small onion, chopped
- 2 tablespoons low-fat margarine
- 2 tablespoons cornstarch
- 2 cups nonfat milk
- 2 cups (16 ounces) low-fat cheddar cheese, shredded
- 2 cups frozen corn, thawed
- 4 eggs, separated
- ¼ teaspoon cream of tartar

## MATERIALS

- Large pot
- Large pan
- Large spoon (for mixing)
- Mixer
- 8 oven-proof, mugs
- Baking sheet

## WHAT TO DO

**1** Preheat oven to 350 degrees.

**2** Cook macaroni 8 minutes in boiling water, until tender; drain.

**3** Sauté onion in margarine until tender.

**4** Add cornstarch and milk to onions; cook and stir until thick and bubbly. Then reduce heat and cook an additional 2 to 3 minutes.

**5** Add cheese and corn to onion mixture, stirring until cheese melts. Remove from heat.

**6** Beat egg yolks and slowly add the cheese and corn mixture, stirring constantly. Then fold macaroni into mixture.

**7** Beat egg whites with cream of tartar until stiff peaks form.

**8** Fill mugs ¼-full with cheese and macaroni mixture. Top with a heaping spoonful of egg white to form clouds.

**9** Place mugs on baking sheet and bake at 350 degrees for 25 to 30 minutes, until golden brown.

**VARIATIONS:** Add other chopped vegetables to the macaroni mixture.

**PRACTICAL TIPS:** Wash and dry mixer blades before beating egg whites. Tell the kids the "clouds" are hot and to eat carefully.

# EAT THE BOWL!

Licking the bowl takes on a whole new meaning with this tasty creation. In fact, why stop at licking? There won't be anything left when the kids are finished—not even the bowl!

• **Serves:** 6        • **Time:** 10 minutes to prepare        • **Complexity:** Easy
                          1½ hours to bake

## INGREDIENTS

- 6 small round or rectangular loaves of French bread
- 1 64-ounce can low-fat, low-salt beef stew, beef stroganoff, macaroni and cheese, or other casserole dish

## MATERIALS

- Knife
- Aluminum foil
- 6 plates
- 6 forks or spoons

## WHAT TO DO

**1** Prepare individual loaves by cutting off the tops and scooping out the insides.

**2** Set excess bread aside for dipping or as a side snack of bread with butter.

**3** Fill the loaves with beef stew or other dish.

**4** Wrap the filled loaves with foil and heat at 325 degrees for 1 to 1½ hours, checking to see whether heated throughout.

**5** When loaves are hot, remove from foil and serve on individual plates.

**6** Hand out forks or spoons and have the guests eat the beef stew first, using the extra bread to dip. When they're finished, they can eat the bowls!

**VARIATIONS:** Fill one large, round sourdough loaf of bread and serve the guests from it. Try other fillers, such as ravioli, chicken casserole, scrambled eggs, pizza toppings, and so on.

**PRACTICAL TIPS:** You can speed up the process by preheating the stew ahead of time. Then heat the entire filled loaf for 20 minutes in the oven. Instead of French bread loaves, you can buy bread bowls already scooped out and ready to be filled. Then simply buy a separate loaf of bread for dipping.

# EDIBLE ANIMALS

How many times do parents tell their kids not to play with their food? Too many! Well, this meal puts an end to all that—you will actually need to encourage your guests to not be shy and to . . . play with their food!

- **Serves:** 6
- **Time:** 20 minutes to prepare
- **Complexity:** Easy

## INGREDIENTS
- 18 slices of whole-wheat bread
- 1 6-ounce can tuna packed in water, drained
- 2 to 3 tablespoons of mayonnaise
- 1 cup low-fat, low-sugar peanut butter
- 1 cup low-sugar jam
- 1 cup low-fat cream cheese
- 1 cup other favorite sandwich spread (optional)
- Sunflower seeds, raisins, or other decorations

## MATERIALS
- Animal-shaped cookie cutters
- Spoons or knives (for spreading)

## WHAT TO DO

**1** Mix tuna with mayonnaise.

**2** Give each guest 3 slices of bread, and let them choose cookie cutters.

**3** Let guests use the cookie cutters to cut out animal shapes, 3 of each animal they chose.

**4** Have the guests spread fillings of their choice onto 2 cutouts and top with a matching cutout.

**5** Have the guests turn the animals upright so they stand up. (The three layers should be enough to make the animal cutouts stand.)

**6** Let the kids play with their food before they eat it!

**VARIATIONS:** Have the bakery tint the bread a variety of colors. Offer a variety of spreads to choose from. Have the guests bring cookie cutters from home to share.

**PRACTICAL TIPS:** Slice the bread lengthwise (or have the bakery slice it for you) instead of the standard way to get more mileage out of the bread. Ask the kids to use their cookie cutters to get as many animals out of their slices as possible.

# HAPPY FACE BURGERS

These Happy Face Burgers have every reason to smile—they cover all four food groups and taste great, making both parents and kids happy.

- **Serves:** 4
- **Time:** 15 minutes to prepare
  20 minutes to cook
- **Complexity:** Easy

## INGREDIENTS

- 1 pound lean ground beef
- ½ cup dry bread crumbs
- 1 package onion soup mix
- ½ cup catsup
- 8 pickle slices
- 4 olives
- 1 tomato, sliced
- 2 cups lettuce, shredded
- Mustard
- 2 whole-wheat hamburger buns or kaiser rolls

## MATERIALS

- Large bowl
- Broiler pan
- 4 plates

## WHAT TO DO

1 Combine ground beef with bread crumbs, soup mix, and catsup in large bowl.

2 Shape into four patties.

3 Broil in oven for 10 minutes on each side.

4 Toast buns or rolls in toaster or under broiler.

5 Place half of each bun (or roll) on individual plates and top with broiled patties to make open-faced sandwiches.

6 Make face, using sliced pickles for eyes, olive for nose, ½ tomato slice for mouth, shredded lettuce for hair, and mustard for eyebrows and pupils.

7 Serve with a smile.

**VARIATION:** Let the guests make their own funny face hamburgers. Just provide condiments for them to use as decorations.

**PRACTICAL TIP:** Keep extra buns or rolls handy in case the kids want to make traditional hamburger sandwiches out of their Happy Face Burgers.

# HEDGE HOG

**W**atch the kids eat a whole Hedge Hog and get their daily supply of fruits and veggies at the same time! You can make the Hog green or purple, whichever your prefer—just don't make it mad! It looks dangerous!

- **Serves:** 8 to 10    • **Time:** 15 to 20 minutes to prepare    • **Complexity:** Easy

## INGREDIENTS

- Small head of cabbage (red or green) or lettuce
- Cherry tomatoes
- Green or purple seedless grapes
- Pineapple chunks
- Strawberries
- Olives, black or green
- Bell pepper chunks, green, yellow, and red
- Carrot rounds
- Celery slices
- Zucchini rounds
- Any other fruit or vegetable you like, cut into bite-sized pieces
- Low-fat ranch dressing and/or low-fat fruit-flavored yogurt

## MATERIALS

- Large plate
- Colored toothpicks or skewers
- Small bowls, 1 for each dip

## WHAT TO DO

**1** To make a foundation for the Hedge Hog, slice bottom off the cabbage or lettuce to create a flat surface. Set on a large plate, flat side down.

**2** Stick toothpicks or skewers all over the cabbage or lettuce to form "quills" for the Hedge Hog.

**3** Stick small pieces of fruits and vegetables onto the quills, enough to cover the whole Hog.

**4** At serving time the guests can pull the quills from the Hedge Hog and eat the fruits and vegetables.

**5** Set out bowls of ranch dressing and/or fruit yogurt for dipping.

**VARIATIONS:** Use cubes of cheese and meat instead of fruit and vegetables. Make the Hedge Hog out of a cantaloupe, melon, or eggplant instead of cabbage or lettuce.

**PRACTICAL TIP:** Collect the toothpicks when finished so the kids don't poke each other with them.

# JURASSIC HATCH

These aren't really dinosaur eggs, but don't tell your guests. Let them pretend that these crazy eggs might be from a Tyrannosaurus Rex!

- **Serves:** 4
- **Time:** 20 minutes to prepare
  30 minutes to cook
- **Complexity:** Easy to Medium

## INGREDIENTS

- 5 eggs
- ½ pound ground, low-fat turkey sausage
- ½ cup low-fat, low-salt crackers (about 20 large crackers), crushed
- Salsa (optional)

## MATERIALS

- Small pan (for boiling eggs)
- Small bowl
- Shallow baking pan

## WHAT TO DO

**1** Preheat oven to 375 degrees.

**2** Boil 4 of the 5 eggs for 15 to 20 minutes.

**3** Run cold water over eggs, crack, and shell carefully.

**4** Divide turkey sausage into 4 portions, and shape each portion into a 4-inch round patty.

**5** Wrap each patty around 1 hard-cooked egg, covering the egg completely.

**6** Beat remaining egg in small bowl.

**7** Roll each sausage-wrapped egg in beaten egg. Then roll in crushed crackers.

**8** Arrange eggs in shallow baking pan and bake for 25 to 30 minutes, until sausage is no longer pink.

**9** Place each egg on individual plate and serve warm or cold, with catsup if desired.

**VARIATIONS:** For added color, but a little more work, hard boil the eggs, then crack them lightly, dip in egg dye to color, and remove shells, leaving a batiklike colored pattern all over eggs. Continue with step 4.

**PRACTICAL TIPS:** To save time, hard boil the eggs ahead of time. Pinch sausage edges to seal the meat around egg.

# KLOWN KIDS

Your guests will have so much fun clowning around with these funny fruit faces, they may not even realize they are eating healthy food!

- **Serves:** 8
- **Time:** 10 minutes to prepare
- **Complexity:** Easy

## INGREDIENTS

- 8 canned pear halves
- 2 cups carrots, shredded
- 16 raisins
- 8 maraschino cherries
- 16 dried or canned apricot halves
- 1 red bell pepper, cut into 8 slices
- 2 cups cottage cheese
- 8 green or purple seedless grapes

## MATERIALS

- 8 plates

## WHAT TO DO

**1** Place 1 pear half on each plate, with wide part at the bottom and narrow part at the top, to form head.

**2** Top with ¼ cup shredded carrots on each clown head for hair.

**3** Use 2 raisins for eyes, 1 cherry for nose, 2 apricot halves for ears, and 1 slice of bell pepper for mouth.

**4** Put a scoop of cottage cheese at bottom for bow, and fill center with 1 grape.

**5** Serve with a smile.

**VARIATION:** Turn the pear sideways to make a puppy dog, using a prune for a floppy ear, a raisin for an eye, a cherry for a nose, and cottage cheese at the bottom for a collar.

**PRACTICAL TIP:** These might be fun to make with the guests, or you might want to surprise them at mealtime by making the Klown Kids ahead of time.

# PAINTED SANDWICHES

Let the little artists create these colorful sandwiches themselves.

- **Serves:** 4
- **Time:** 20 minutes to prepare
  10 minutes to cook
- **Complexity:** Easy

## INGREDIENTS

- 8 slices whole-wheat bread
- 8 tablespoons low-fat margarine or spread
- Food coloring, red, blue, green, and yellow
- 4 slices favorite cheese

## MATERIALS

- Paper towels
- 4 small bowls
- 4 small paintbrushes
- Frying pan
- 4 small plates

## WHAT TO DO

**1** Allow margarine or spread to soften. Then divide into 4 bowls.

**2** Mix a different food coloring into each bowl of margarine.

**3** Give each guest 2 slices of whole-wheat bread on a paper towel and 1 paintbrush.

**4** Have the guests use their paintbrushes to paint the tops of both slices of bread with the tinted margarine.

**5** Place a slice of cheese on the uncolored side of bread, and cover with second slice of bread, colored side up.

**6** Grill in frying pan for 5 minutes on each side, until lightly browned.

**7** Serve works of art on individual plates.

**VARIATIONS:** Add other spreads, such as tuna, slices of low-fat ham, or turkey, inside the sandwich.

**PRACTICAL TIP:** Use light whole-wheat bread so colors show up well.

# PEANUT BUTTER BURGER DOGS

Give those hamburger patties a peanutty taste and a hot dog shape, and beef up the protein as well as the flavor.

- **Serves:** 4
- **Time:** 20 minutes to prepare
  8 minutes to cook
- **Complexity:** Easy

## INGREDIENTS

- 2 eggs, slightly beaten
- 1 pound lean ground beef
- ¼ cup onion, chopped
- ¼ cup chunky peanut butter
- 4 whole-wheat hot dog buns
- Condiments (catsup, mustard, pickles, and so on)

## MATERIALS

- Large bowl
- Broiler pan
- Broiler

## WHAT TO DO

**1** Combine eggs, ground beef, onion, and peanut butter in bowl and mix well.

**2** Shape mixture into four long patties, the length of the hot dog buns.

**3** Broil 6 to 8 minutes on each side, until browned and cooked.

**4** Place each Burger Dog on a whole-wheat hot dog bun, and serve with condiments.

**VARIATION:** Shape into rounds and serve on hamburger buns.

**PRACTICAL TIP:** Combining the ingredients with your hands makes it easy to shape the mixture.

# PERSONALIZED PIZZA FACE

Here's how to make a Personalized Pizza Face, complete with the guests' names!

- **Serves:** 4
- **Time:** 20 minutes to prepare
  15 minutes to bake
- **Complexity:** Easy

## INGREDIENTS

- 1 8-ounce package refrigerated pizza dough
- 1 12-ounce jar pizza sauce
- 1 cup mozzarella cheese, shredded
- 1 cup cheddar cheese, shredded
- 1 zucchini, cut into circles
- 4 black olives, pitted, cut in half
- 2 cherry tomatoes, cut in half
- 1 red, 1 green, and 1 yellow bell pepper (or all the same color) cut into thin slices

## MATERIALS

- Cookie sheet or 4 individual pizza pans

## WHAT TO DO

**1** Divide refrigerator dough into 4 parts.

**2** Shape each quarter into a circle to form mini-sized pizzas.

**3** Pour equal amounts of pizza sauce over the 4 circles.

**4** Sprinkle equal amounts of mozzarella cheese over each of the four circles.

**5** Make pizza face, using zucchini wheels for eyes olive halves as pupils inside eyes, cherry tomatoes for noses, and bell pepper slices for smiles.

**6** Use remaining pepper slices to write the guests' names on each pizza.

**7** Bake according to package directions, until hot and bubbly.

**8** Remove from oven and sprinkle cheddar cheese at the top for hair.

**VARIATIONS:** Make a large pizza with one big pizza face. If you make this meal for a birthday, write "Happy Birthday" or the birthday child's name at the bottom, using the bell pepper slices.

**PRACTICAL TIPS:** Leave room at the bottom of the pizza face to write the names. Cut the bell peppers into pieces small enough to use for lettering.

# PIZZA PINWHEELS

Here's a new way to enjoy an old favorite. We've given the pizza a whole new look!

- **Serves:** 8
- **Time:** 20 minutes to prepare
  20 minutes to bake
- **Complexity:** Easy

## INGREDIENTS
- 1 8-ounce can refrigerated crescent rolls
- 1 cup pizza or spaghetti sauce
- 1 cup mozzarella cheese, grated
- 1 cup pizza toppings, such as bell peppers, mushrooms, olives, low-fat salami, low-fat ham, or any combination, finely chopped

## MATERIALS
- Knife
- Cookie sheet

## WHAT TO DO

**1** Preheat oven to 350 degrees.

**2** Separate dough into 4 rectangles at their perforation marks and press the triangle perforations together to make a smooth surface.

**3** Top with a thin layer of pizza or spaghetti sauce. Then sprinkle cheese and finely chopped toppings on top.

**4** Starting at shorter side, lightly roll up each rectangle and pinch along loose edge to seal.

**5** Slice each roll into 4 equal parts.

**6** Pinch dough together on one side of each slice to seal. Place sealed-side down on ungreased cookie sheet.

**7** Bake at 350 degrees for 18 to 20 minutes, until golden brown.

**8** Serve 2 to each guest.

**VARIATION:** Before baking, sprinkle additional sauce and cheese on top of the pinwheels.

**PRACTICAL TIP:** Be sure to pinch ends closed so the rolls won't fall apart while baking.

# POTATO PACKERS

The classic baked potato becomes a whole meal when you offer these creative tater toppers on the side. Let the kids pick and choose what they want on top!

- **Serves:** 8
- **Time:** 15 minutes to prepare
  1 hour to cook
- **Complexity:** Easy

## INGREDIENTS

- 8 medium potatoes
- 8 tablespoons low-fat margarine, softened
- 1 cup low-fat cheese, grated
- 1 cup fat-free sour cream
- 2 cups low-fat chili
- 1 cup low-fat ground beef, cooked in taco seasoning and crumbled; OR
  8 strips of lean bacon, cooked and crumbled; OR
  1 cup low-fat baked ham, cubed
- 1 small bag low-fat, low-salt tortilla chips, crumbled
- ½ cup green onion, chopped (optional)
- ½ cup Parmesan cheese (optional)

## MATERIALS

- Aluminum foil
- Small bowls, 1 for each topping
- 8 plates
- 9 forks

## WHAT TO DO

**1** Preheat oven to 400 degrees.

**2** Pierce potatoes with fork, wrap in foil, and bake for 1 hour at 400 degrees, until tender.

**3** While potatoes are baking, prepare and arrange toppings in small bowls on counter or table.

**4** When the potatoes are done, place them on individual plates, cut open, and pinch sides to puff up.

**5** Have guests walk around buffet-style to select toppings.

**VARIATIONS:** For a vegetarian meal, omit the meat and offer a variety of low-fat cheeses or a number of vegetables. Or top the potatoes with melted cheese, beef stroganoff sauce, spaghetti sauce, or other casserole sauce.

**PRACTICAL TIP:** Pinching the potatoes open helps them cool more quickly, so your guests can eat them more easily.

# RAINBOW JELL-O

This beautiful layered dish is full of surprises. Just match the Jell-O to the fruit or veggie to create your special rainbow!

- **Serves:** 8
- **Time:** 20 minutes to prepare
  3 hours to set
- **Complexity:** Easy

## INGREDIENTS

- 6-ounce package orange Jell-O
- 1 cup carrots, shredded, or peaches, cubed
- 6-ounce package lemon Jell-O
- 1 cup zucchini, shredded, or banana, cubed
- 6-ounce package lime Jell-O
- 1 cup frozen peas or green grapes
- 6-ounce package strawberry Jell-O
- 1 cup red apple, shredded, or strawberries, chopped

## MATERIALS

- Mixing bowl
- Large clear-glass baking pan or large bowl
- 8 serving bowls
- 8 spoons

## WHAT TO DO

**1** Prepare orange Jell-O according to package directions.

**2** Pour liquid into pan or bowl.

**3** Stir in matching veggie or fruit.

**4** Place in refrigerator and allow to set until firm, at least 1 hour.

**5** Repeat steps 1 through 4 with remaining 3 flavors of Jell-O, allowing each layer time to set before adding the next layer.

**6** Show off the Rainbow; spoon into individual bowls and serve.

**VARIATIONS:** Add a layer of low-fat sour cream between Jell-O layers, and frost the top with a layer of sour cream or low-fat whipped cream.

**PRACTICAL TIPS:** Begin preparing this treat early in the day or a day before the party, and be sure to allow each layer to firm up before adding the next layer.

# SPAGHETTI PIE

Take a favorite meal and turn it into a fun-to-eat pie.

- **Serves:** 8
- **Time:** 20 minutes to prepare
  20 minutes to bake
- **Complexity:** Easy

## Ingredients

- 6 ounces of spaghetti
- 2 tablespoons low-fat margarine
- 2 eggs
- ⅓ cup low-fat, low-salt Parmesan cheese
- Vegetable spray
- 1 12-ounce jar favorite spaghetti sauce
- 1 cup low-fat cheddar cheese, grated

## Materials

- Large pot
- Large bowl
- Mixer or whisk
- Pie pan
- 8 plates

## What To Do

1. Cook spaghetti in large pot of water according to package directions. Then drain, pour into bowl, and stir in margarine.

2. Preheat oven to 350 degrees.

3. Beat eggs. Stir Parmesan cheese into eggs.

4. Spray pie pan with vegetable spray, and spread spaghetti in pan to form "crust."

5. Pour spaghetti sauce over spaghetti, and sprinkle cheddar cheese and the egg mixture over the top.

6. Bake at 350 degrees for 20 minutes.

7. Serve in slices on individual plates.

**Variations:** Add meat to the spaghetti sauce. Use macaroni, fettuccine, or angel-hair pasta. Try adding jack or mozzarella cheese with the cheddar cheese.

**Practical Tip:** Use a deep-dish pie pan if you have one.

# SPEAR-FISHING DIP

Outfit your guests with miniature spears and have them go fishing in the cheesy quicksand. They may not find anything, but they'll sure have fun trying!

- **Serves:** 8
- **Time:** 20 minutes to prepare
- **Complexity:** Easy

## INGREDIENTS

- ½ pound low-fat Gruyere cheese, shredded
- ½ pound low-fat Emmentaler cheese (or use any low-fat cheeses you like, but these are sweet, melt easily, and taste delicious), shredded
- 1½ tablespoons cornstarch
- 1 teaspoon dry mustard
- ½ teaspoon garlic salt
- 1 12-ounce can clear, sugar-free soda
- 1 tablespoon lemon juice
- 1 loaf French bread, cut into cubes

## MATERIALS

- Medium mixing bowl
- Heavy pan or fondue pot
- Serving dish
- Wooden spoon
- 8 fondue forks or wooden skewers

## WHAT TO DO

**1** Mix cheese with cornstarch, mustard, and garlic salt in medium bowl.

**2** Heat soda and lemon juice in heavy pan or fondue pot over medium heat.

**3** When bubbles start to rise, add cheese mixture a spoonful at a time and stir in a figure-eight pattern with a wooden spoon until cheese is melted and smooth.

**4** Pour into serving dish and set on table.

**5** Serve with bread cubes and "spears" (fondue forks or skewers).

**VARIATIONS:** Use cheddar cheese for a change of taste. Offer the guests veggies, as well as bread cubes, to dip into the cheese.

**PRACTICAL TIP:** If you have a heating tray, use it to keep the melted cheese warm.

# SURPRISE INSIDE

What looks like a plain old dinner roll turns out to be a whole meal! That's the surprise inside!

- **Serves:** 4
- **Time:** 15 minutes to prepare
  20 minutes to bake
- **Complexity:** Easy

## INGREDIENTS

- ½ pound lean ground beef
- ¼ cup onion, chopped
- 1 12-ounce jar pizza sauce
- 2 tablespoons olives, chopped
- 1 teaspoon dried basil, crushed
- ½ teaspoon dried oregano, crushed
- 4 individual French rolls, about 8 inches long
- 2 cups mozzarella cheese, shredded

## MATERIALS

- Frying pan
- Spoon
- Knife
- Aluminum foil

## WHAT TO DO

1 Cook meat and onion until meat is brown; drain off grease.

2 Stir in pizza sauce, olives, and seasonings.

3 Preheat oven to 375 degrees.

4 Cut rolls in half lengthwise and hollow out insides to within ½ inch of edges.

5 Sprinkle half the cheese into the bottom half of each roll.

6 Spoon meat mixture over cheese.

7 Sprinkle remaining cheese on top of meat.

8 Place roll tops on top to cover the mixture.

9 Wrap each roll in foil and bake at 375 degrees for 20 minutes.

**VARIATIONS:** Substitute cubes of lean ham for ground beef. Use other cheeses besides mozzarella.

**PRACTICAL TIP:** Tell the guests the rolls are hot and to eat them carefully.

# TWINKLE SANDWICH

Make these star-shaped sandwiches for your under-the-sea or under-the-sky parties!

- **Serves:** 6
- **Time:** 15 minutes to prepare
- **Complexity:** Easy

## INGREDIENTS

- 3 loaves whole-wheat bread, one tinted pink, another yellow, and the third blue
- 1 cup low-fat, low-sugar peanut butter
- 1 cup low-sugar jelly
- 2 cups trail mix, raisins, or other snack

## MATERIALS

- Knife
- 6 plates

## WHAT TO DO

**1** Special order tinted bread from the bakery, sliced into thin sandwich slices.

**2** Trim off the crust and make peanut butter and jelly sandwiches or other favorite sandwiches.

**3** Cut sandwiches diagonally into four triangles.

**4** Place five triangles on a plate to form a star.

**5** Fill the centers of the stars with trail mix or other favorite snacks.

**VARIATIONS:** You can make the sandwiches all one color, alternate the colors, or make triple-deckers that have all three colors in one.

**PRACTICAL TIP:** Be sure to special order the bread several days before the party so it's ready in time.

# CREATIVE CAKES

The fancy celebration cake is truly the icing on the party. The cake can serve as a decorative centerpiece, or it can make a surprise entrance at the perfect time.

When making birthday and holiday cakes, you can make them more nutritious by using angel food, chiffon, or carrot cake mixes or recipes, or by adding bran, whole-wheat flour, and pureed vegetables or fruits to your recipes. If you prefer to use store-bought cakes or mixes, look for low-fat, low-sugar cakes. Instead of using high-sugar frosting, try low-fat cream cheese spreads, low-sugar jams, or pureed fruit for frosting, and use frosting tubes sparingly to decorate. Then top the cake with plastic dinosaurs, small dolls, fancy candles, beautiful flowers, or other toys for a festive presentation.

You can turn the cake decoration into a party activity by letting your guests participate: give them cupcakes or individual slices, or have them work on the whole cake. Then light the candles and sing "Happy Birthday!"

# Animal Cakes

**W**ith a little imagination, you can make any animal you want. Ours is a rabbit, but it could be a cat, mouse, dog, turtle, or even a dinosaur!

- **Serves:** 10
- **Time:** 10 minutes to prepare
  20 minutes to decorate
  30 minutes to bake
- **Complexity:** Easy

## Ingredients
- Angel food or chiffon cake mix
- 2 cans low-fat cream cheese frosting (or see our recipe on page 211)
- Food coloring, appropriate for the animal you are making
- Ladyfingers, wafer cookies, graham crackers, or other cookies
- Coconut, decorative sprinkles, candies, fruits, or nuts
- Thin licorice strips
- Vegetable spray

## Materials
- Small oven-proof bowl
- Medium oven-proof bowl
- Large piece of cardboard covered with aluminum foil
- Tubes of frosting with decorator tips (optional)

## What To Do

**1** Prepare cake mix and pour into the medium and small bowls sprayed with vegetable spray.

**2** Bake until done, cool, remove from bowls, and set small cake next to large cake, flat sides down, on the foil-covered cardboard.

**3** Cut out two small holes in smaller cake where ears should be and insert ladyfingers. Place half a ladyfinger behind larger cake for tail.

**4** Tint the frosting with food coloring.

**5** Spread frosting over both round cakes and ladyfingers.

**6** Tint coconut with food coloring and sprinkle over cakes.

**7** Add eyes, nose, whiskers, and so on, with decorative additions.

**Variations:** Make a cat by using wafer cookies for ears and a long ladyfinger tail. Make a mouse by using licorice for whiskers and tail, and round cookies for ears. Make a stegosaur by using wafer cookies for spikes and ladyfingers for a long tail and half ladyfingers for feet.

**Practical Tip:** Cake batter in bowls may take longer to bake than package or recipe derections indicate. Cakes are done when a toothpick inserted into center comes out clean.

# BOTTOMS-UP CAKES

These black-and-white Bottoms-Up Cakes are filled with a delicious surprise center!

- **Serves:** Makes 24 cupcakes
- **Time:** 15 minutes to prepare 25 minutes to bake
- **Complexity:** Easy

## INGREDIENTS

- 1 8-ounce package low-fat cream cheese, softened
- ¼ cup powdered sugar
- 1 egg
- 1 6-ounce package chocolate or carob chips
- 1 package low-fat chocolate cake mix
- 24 maraschino cherries, chocolate kisses, or whole walnuts

## MATERIALS

- Mixer
- Spoon
- Cupcake tin
- Paper or foil cupcake liners

## WHAT TO DO

1. Mix cream cheese, sugar, and egg together until well blended.

2. Stir chocolate or carob chips into cream cheese mixture. Set aside.

3. Prepare cake mix, line cupcake tin with cupcake liners, and fill each half full.

4. Drop a heaping teaspoon of cream cheese mixture in the center of each cupcake.

5. Press a cherry, chocolate kiss, or walnut into the center of the cream cheese.

6. Place cupcake tin in oven, and bake at 350 degrees for 25 to 30 minutes.

**VARIATIONS:** Divide the cream cheese mixture into 4 parts and tint each part a different color for an added surprise. Add other goodies, such as Reese's Pieces, chopped nuts, raisins, or candy, to the cream cheese mixture.

**PRACTICAL TIP:** These cupcakes are so moist, they don't need to be frosted, but you can frost them if you like.

# CREEPY CATERPILLAR CAKE

**W**atch this Creepy Caterpillar Cake crawl all over the table—and into the mouths of your hungry guests.

- **Serves:** 12
- **Time:** 10 minutes to prepare
  20 minutes to bake
  20 minutes to decorate
- **Complexity:** Easy

## INGREDIENTS

- Angel food, carrot, or favorite low-fat cake mix
- Vegetable spray
- 3 cans low-fat cream cheese frosting (or see page 211 for our recipe)
- Food coloring, green
- 1 cup coconut
- Decorative sprinkles, candies, and raisins

## MATERIALS

- Cupcake tin
- Large plastic bag
- 26 pipe cleaners

## WHAT TO DO

**1** Prepare cake batter according to package directions, tint green, and pour into cupcake tin sprayed with vegetable spray.

**2** Bake according to package directions, remove from oven, and cool.

**3** Tint the cream cheese frosting green.

**4** Place coconut in large plastic bag with a few drops of green food coloring and shake well until coconut is tinted green.

**5** Give each guest a cupcake, some frosting, coconut, and decorative candies to decorate their cupcakes.

**6** Give each guest 2 pipe cleaners. Have them bend the pipe cleaners 90 degrees and stick one end into each side of the cupcake, with the other end pointing down to form legs.

**7** Set the cupcakes next to one another in a long, wavy line to form a giant caterpillar. (The cupcakes don't have to be connected—they rest on their bottoms with the legs sticking out on the sides.)

**8** Add two raisins to the front cupcake to make eyes, and stick 2 pipe cleaners on top to make antennae.

**VARIATIONS:** Decorate the cupcakes with different colors of cream cheese frosting to make a snake, a crocodile, a worm, or a funny-looking critter.

**PRACTICAL TIPS:** Spray cupcake tin generously with vegetable spray so cupcakes are easy to remove. Cut pipe cleaners in half for smaller legs.

# BUTTERFLY CAKE

This fancy cake is so colorful and cute, yet so delicious and easy to make!

- **Serves:** 10
- **Time:** 10 minutes to prepare
  30 minutes to bake
  20 minutes to decorate
- **Complexity:** Easy

## INGREDIENTS
- 1 package angel food or white cake mix
- Vegetable spray
- Food coloring, yellow and other colors
- 4 ladyfingers
- 2 cans low-fat cream cheese frosting (or see page 211 for our recipe)
- Decorative sprinkles, small candies, dried fruit, or nuts
- 1 thin strip of licorice

## MATERIALS
- Round cake pan
- Toothpicks
- Knife
- Large serving plate

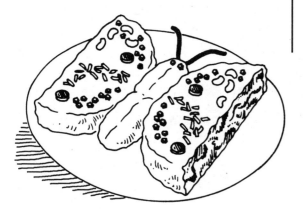

## WHAT TO DO

**1** Prepare cake mix according to package directions and pour into round pan sprayed with vegetable spray.

**2** Squeeze a few drops of several food colors into batter; swirl with toothpicks.

**3** Bake according to package directions, cool, remove from pan, and cut cake in half vertically.

**4** Set cake on plate with round sides together and flat centers facing out, to form butterfly wings.

**5** Place 4 ladyfingers between the round sides, 2 above and 2 below where the halves of the cake meet, to form butterfly body.

**6** Tint the cream cheese frosting yellow and cover cake with frosting—everywhere but flat sides, where the colorful swirls in the batter are visible.

**7** Decorate with sprinkles, candies, dried fruit, nuts, and so on.

**8** Cut thin licorice in half, curl up ends, fold in half, and place on top of top ladyfinger to make antennae.

**VARIATION:** Have your guests make their own individual butterflies, using cupcakes instead of whole cake.

**PRACTICAL TIP:** Cut up dried fruits for a healthier alternative to candies, and place them in a creative design to simulate butterfly markings.

# CRISPY CAKE

This cake has an unexpected crunch that will delight your guests.

- **Serves:** 10
- **Time:** 20 minute to prepare 30 minutes to set
- **Complexity:** Easy

## INGREDIENTS

- 1 large bag marshmallows
- ¾ cup low-fat margarine
- 6 cups Rice Krispies or popped popcorn
- 2 cups Gummy Bears or sugar-free gumdrops
- 2 cups peanuts, chopped
- Vegetable spray

## MATERIALS

- Large saucepan
- Spoon
- Angel-food-cake pan

## WHAT TO DO

**1** In large saucepan, melt marshmallows and margarine over medium heat until well blended.

**2** Stir in cereal or popcorn, candies, and nuts; mix well.

**3** Pour the mixture into an angel-food-cake pan sprayed with vegetable spray and press down.

**4** Cool, remove from pan, and serve.

**5** Decorate if desired.

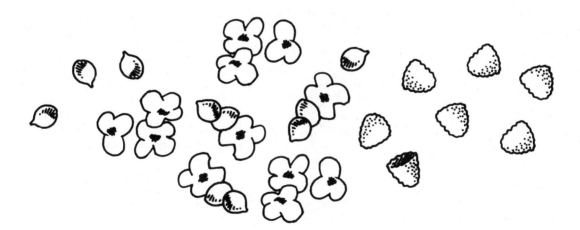

**VARIATIONS:** Use a rectangular pan and decorate as you would any other cake with cream cheese frosting and decorator tubes. Or press into cupcake tin for individual servings.

**PRACTICAL TIP:** Stir in cereal or popcorn, candies, and nuts quickly, before hot mixture cools.

# MERRY-GO-ROUND CAKE

If you're hosting a carnival, circus, or fair party, the Merry-Go-Round Cake makes a perfect centerpiece and a delicious treat. Decorate the cake with tiny toys the kids can take home.

- **Serves:** 8 to 10
- **Time:** 10 minutes to prepare
  30 minutes to bake
  20 minutes to decorate
- **Complexity:** Moderate

## INGREDIENTS

- 1 package low-fat, low-sugar angel food or chiffon cake mix
- Vegetable spray
- 2 cans low-fat cream cheese frosting (or see page 211 for our recipe)
- 1 cup low-sugar strawberry or other flavor jam
- Tubes of frosting with decorator tips

## MATERIALS

- 2 round cake pans
- Tiny plastic horses, animals, people, clowns, and/or vehicles
- 8 wooden dowels, painted bright colors with nontoxic paint
- 1 aluminum, plastic, or metal pie pan

## WHAT TO DO

1. Prepare the cake mix, pour into 2 round cake pans sprayed with vegetable spray, and bake according to package directions. When cake is done, remove from cake pan and cool completely.

2. Spread frosting on top of 1 cake and top with a layer of jam.

3. Place second cake on top or frosted cake and cover with frosting, reserving ½ cup.

4. Using decorator tubes, pipe frosting decorations around bottom and top borders and along sides of cake, making stars, balls, leaves, and so on.

5. Place tiny plastic horses, animals, or other small toys on top of cake.

6. Insert dowels around the top border to hold aluminum, plastic, or metal pie pan.

7. Frost pie pan with remaining frosting and decorate with decorator tubes.

8. Dot tops of dowels with frosting. Then set pan on top to make roof.

# Creative Cakes

**VARIATIONS:**  Omit the roof and create other scenarios, such as a dinosaur land, a farmyard, or a beach, using plastic figures.

**PRACTICAL TIP:**  Be sure to remind your guests that the plastic toys on top are not edible!

# CUPCAKE CLOWNS

Cupcake Clowns are always popular at parties. Instead of buying them at the ice-cream store, you can make this fun party treat yourself. Better yet, have your guests create their own one-of-a-kind clowns!

- **Serves:** 12
- **Time:** 10 minutes to prepare
  20 minutes to bake
  20 minutes to decorate
- **Complexity:** Easy

## INGREDIENTS

- 1 package low-fat carrot cake mix or low-fat blueberry muffin mix
- ½ gallon low-fat frozen vanilla yogurt
- 2 cans low-fat cream cheese frosting (or see page 211 for our recipe)
- Tubes of frosting with decorator tips
- Small candies, seeds, nuts, or raisins.
- 12 ice-cream cones
- 12 maraschino cherries

## MATERIALS

- 12 paper or foil cupcake liners
- Cupcake tin
- 12 medium plates

## WHAT TO DO

**1** Prepare cake or muffin mix according to package directions.

**2** Place 12 cupcake liners in cupcake tin and fill each half full with batter.

**3** Bake according to package directions; remove from cupcake tin, and cool.

**4** Spread open paper liners and set each cupcake on a separate plate.

**5** Frost the cupcakes with cream cheese frosting and create a face using frosting tubes, candies, nuts, seeds, and other decorations.

**6** Fill ice-cream cone with ball of frozen yogurt level with top of cone, and place upside down on top of frosted cupcake to make a hat.

**7** Decorate the cone hat with dots of frosting and place a cherry on top, secured with a dot of frosting on tip of cone.

**VARIATION:** Tint the cupcake batter to make the clowns a variety of colors inside.

**PRACTICAL TIPS:** If you have trouble keeping the clown's hat on, stick a toothpick into the cupcake to keep the hat upright.

# DOLL-IN-THE-CAKE

What a surprise your guests will have when they see this Doll-in-the-Cake dessert. Just don't bake the doll!

- **Serves:** 8 to 10
- **Time:** 10 minutes to prepare
  30 minutes to bake
  20 minutes to decorate
- **Complexity:** Easy

## INGREDIENTS

- 1 package low-fat angel food, chiffon, or carrot cake mix
- Vegetable spray
- 2 cans low-fat cream cheese frosting (or see page 211 for our recipe)
- Tubes of frosting with decorator tips
- Tiny candy decorations (optional)

## MATERIALS

- Medium-sized, round, oven-proof bowl
- Toothpick
- Large serving plate
- 1 small 8-to-12-inch doll or action figure

## WHAT TO DO

**1** Mix cake according to package directions.

**2** Spray vegetable spray inside bowl and pour in batter to ¾ full.

**3** Bake a little longer than package directions; test with toothpick.

**4** Cool, remove from bowl, and place flat side down on serving plate.

**5** Push doll, feet first, into cake until top reaches doll's waist.

**6** Decorate cake with a layer of frosting.

**7** Using frosting tubes, make stars, hearts, balls, or other designs to create a ball gown. Add tiny candy decorations if you like.

**8** After serving the cake, wash the doll and give to the guest of honor.

**VARIATIONS:** Make the cake a mountain or volcano and have small animals, dinosaurs, or action figures crawling out of the top. Tint frosting for color.

**PRACTICAL TIP:** If you prefer not to bake a cake, use an angel food cake with a hole in the center.

# EARTH CAKE

Make a journey to the center of the Earth with this multilayered geological discovery.

- **Serves:** 10
- **Time:** 10 minutes to prepare
  30 minutes to bake
  20 minute to decorate
  4 hours to freeze
- **Complexity:** Easy

## INGREDIENTS

- 1 package low-fat carrot cake mix
- Vegetable spray
- 1 pint favorite flavor low-fat frozen yogurt, softened
- 2 cans low-fat cream cheese frosting (or see page 211 for our recipe)
- Food coloring, green and blue
- ½ cup coconut, toasted
- ½ cup coconut, tinted green
- ½ cup pineapple or other fruit, chopped

## MATERIALS

- Large oven-proof bowl
- Toothpick
- Ice-cream scoop or spoon
- Platter
- Miniature plastic trees, houses, or other Earth items

## WHAT TO DO

1 Prepare cake mix according to package directions and pour into large bowl sprayed with vegetable spray.

2 Bake a little longer than package directions; test with toothpick. Cool.

3 Hollow out the inside, leaving a 2-inch lining of cake and scoop softened frozen yogurt into the hollow.

4 Make a small hole in the center of the frozen yogurt and place chopped fruit inside.

5 Freeze for 4 hours or more. Then turn onto platter and remove bowl.

6 Tint cream cheese frosting blue. Frost the cake to form "ocean."

7 Sprinkle brown and green coconut over frosting to make earth patterns. Decorate with miniature trees, houses, spacecrafts, and so on.

**VARIATIONS:** You can decorate the round cake into anything you like—a basketball, a volcano, a face, a moon, an igloo, or whatever.

**PRACTICAL TIP:** Cake is done when a toothpick inserted into center comes out clean.

# Fancy Flower Cake

Delight your guests with a beautiful flower garden that hides a surprise inside. Tell them to eat carefully so they don't miss the treat!

- **Serves:** 12
- **Time:** 10 minutes to prepare
  30 minutes to bake
  20 minutes decoration
- **Complexity:** Moderate

## Ingredients

- 1 package low-fat angel food, chiffon, or carrot cake mix
- Vegetable spray
- 2 cans low-fat cream cheese frosting (or see page 211 for our recipe)

## Materials

- Sheet-cake pan
- Knife
- Spoon
- Gummy Worms, small toys (too large to swallow!), or small candies
- Cardboard as large as the sheet-cake pan, wrapped with aluminum foil
- Real, edible flowers or candy flowers
- 12 plates

## What To Do

1. Prepare cake according to package directions and bake cake in a sheet-cake pan sprayed with vegetable spray. Cool cake in pan.

2. Slice cake into enough pieces for guests.

3. Scoop out a small amount of cake in the center of each piece with a spoon and insert a Gummy Worm, candy, or toy in hole.

4. Place foil-wrapped cardboard on top of cake and flip the cake over carefully, keeping all slices together.

5. Gently remove pan, leaving the cake on top of the cardboard.

6. Frost with cream cheese frosting.

7. Decorate each piece with real, edible flowers or with candy flowers.

8. Serve cake slices on individual plates and let each guest discover a wormy surprise.

**Variations:** Instead of decorating with flowers, decorate cake with decorating tubes. Tint the cream cheese frosting any color you like.

**Practical Tip:** Edible flowers are available at gourmet food stores.

# HAPPY HAMBURGER CAKE

A hamburger for dessert? Sure! This Happy Hamburger Cake will give your party plenty of personality!

- **Serves:** 10
- **Time:** 10 minutes to prepare
  30 minutes to bake
  20 minutes to decorate
- **Complexity:** Moderate

## INGREDIENTS

- 1 pint chocolate low-fat frozen yogurt, softened
- 1 package white or yellow cake mix
- Vegetable spray
- 1 can low-sugar milk chocolate frosting
- 1 tube each red, green, and yellow frosting
- Slivered almonds
- 2 large marshmallows

## MATERIALS

- Oven-proof bowl with rounded bottom
- 2 round cake pans
- 2 large serving plates
- Toothpicks

## WHAT TO DO

**1** Spread softened frozen yogurt in 1 cake pan and refreeze.

**2** Prepare cake mix according to package directions and divide batter between oven-proof bowl and 1 cake pan, both sprayed with vegetable spray.

**3** Bake according to package directions, turn out cakes onto large serving plate, and cool.

**4** Frost sides of cake with chocolate frosting.

**5** Squirt green frosting rounds along the top edge of the cake, to form pickles.

**6** Place cake from bowl, flat side down, on second plate. Frost with chocolate frosting and sprinkle on slivered almonds, to make bun top.

**7** Stick toothpicks into marshmallows and onto side of rounded cake, to form a pair of eyes. Dot centers of eyes with icing to form pupils.

**8** Remove frozen yogurt from pan and place on flat cake to make a hamburger patty.

# Creative Cakes

**9** Squirt red and yellow frosting on yog̲ form catsup and mustard.

**10** Top with rounded cake to form Happy Hamburger Face.

**VARIATION:** Make mini-sized hamburgers, using cupcakes for individual servings.

**PRACTICAL TIP:** You can bake the whole cake in an oven-proof bowl and simply cut it in half when you're ready to create the hamburger bun.

# GINGERCAKE HOUSE

gerbread house but it's really a gingerbread cake—and you can eat the whole
cardboard!). Let the kids help!

- **Time:** 10 minutes to prepare
  30 minutes to bake
  30 minutes to decorate

- **Complexity:** Easy

## INGREDIENTS

- 1 package gingerbread cake mix
- Vegetable spray
- 2 cans low-fat cream cheese frosting (or see page 211 for our recipe)
- 4 whole graham crackers
- Tubes of frosting with decorator tips
- Sprinkles, small candies, cookies, dried fruit, nuts, and other edible decorations

## MATERIALS

- Square pan
- Square sheet of cardboard, slightly larger than cake pan, wrapped with aluminum foil
- Large sheet of tagboard or cardboard
- Pair of scissors

## WHAT TO DO

**1** Prepare cake mix according to package directions and pour into square pan sprayed with vegetable spray; bake.

**2** Remove cake from pan and place on foil-wrapped cardboard square.

**3** Cut tagboard or cardboard into a long rectangle and bend in the center to form roof for house. Trim to fit cake.

**4** Frost roof and attach graham crackers to make shingles.

**5** Frost cake and set roof on top.

**6** Let the kids decorate the Gingercake House with edible decorations, creating doors, windows, and trim.

**7** Admire the Gingercake House, then gobble it up before the witch does.

**VARIATION:** You can frost the graham cracker shingles too. Then let the kids add decorations to them.

**PRACTICAL TIP:** Stick a couple of lollipops or peppermint sticks under roof for support.

# Ice-Cream Cone Cakes

These magical Ice-Cream Cone Cakes combine the fun of ice-cream cones and the festivity of cake.

- **Serves:** 18
- **Time:** 10 minutes to prepare
  12 to 15 minutes to bake
  20 minutes to decorate
- **Complexity:** Easy

## Ingredients

- 1 package low-fat angel food or carrot cake mix
- Food coloring, variety of colors
- 18 waffle-style ice-cream cones with flat bottoms
- 1 can low-fat cream cheese frosting (or see page 211 for our recipe)
- Candy sprinkles

## Materials

- Cupcake tins
- Toothpick

## What To Do

**1** Make cake mix according to package directions.

**2** Fill each cone half full with batter and set in cupcake tin.

**3** Squeeze a few drops of different food colors into each cone and swirl batter with toothpick.

**4** Bake at 350 degrees for 12 to 15 minutes, remove from oven, and cool completely.

**5** Tint cream cheese frosting with pastel food colors to look like sherbets.

**6** Frost cupcake cones with different colors of frosting.

**7** Sprinkle candy sprinkles on top.

**Variation:** Use a low-fat muffin mix for a more nutritious dessert.

**Practical Tip:** Use foil around the bottom of cones to keep them from tipping over.

# JOHNNY APPLESEED CAKE

This delicious cake is low in sugar, high in oats and apples, and covers three food groups—but your guests don't have to know that!.

- **Serves:** 8
- **Time:** 20 minutes to prepare
  35 minutes to bake
- **Complexity:** Easy

## INGREDIENTS

- 4 cups baking apples (about 6 medium apples), sliced
- Vegetable spray
- ½ cup brown sugar
- ½ cup flour
- ¾ rolled oats
- ¾ teaspoon cinnamon
- ¾ teaspoon nutmeg
- ⅓ cup low-fat margarine, cut into little pieces
- Low-fat, low-sugar whipped topping

## MATERIALS

- 8-inch square pan
- Medium mixing bowl

## WHAT TO DO

**1** Preheat oven to 350 degrees.

**2** Place sliced apples into pan sprayed with vegetable spray.

**3** Blend brown sugar, flour, oats, spices, and margarine together until crumbly. Spread over apples.

**4** Bake at 350 degrees for 35 minutes, until topping is golden brown.

**5** Top with sugar-free whipped topping.

**VARIATIONS:** Frost cake with cream cheese frosting and decorate to fit the theme. Or top with low-fat frozen yogurt.

**PRACTICAL TIP:** Double the recipe and bake in larger pan for more or bigger servings.

# OVER-THE-RAINBOW CAKE

**S**omewhere over the rainbow you'll find this stunning centerpiece cake!

- **Serves:** 10
- **Time:** 10 minutes to prepare
  30 minutes to bake
  20 minutes to decorate
- **Complexity:** Easy

## INGREDIENTS

- 1 package low-fat angel food or white cake mix
- Vegetable spray
- Food coloring, any colors
- 2 cans low-fat cream cheese frosting (or see page 211 for our recipe)
- Tubes of frosting (red, orange, yellow, blue, and green)

## MATERIALS

- 2 round cake pans
- Toothpicks
- Knife
- Star-shaped decorator tip
- Candles

## WHAT TO DO

1 Prepare cake mix according to package directions and pour into round pans sprayed with vegetable spray.

2 Squeeze several food colors into batter and swirl with toothpick.

3 Bake according to package directions, cool, remove from pans, and cut each round cake in half to form 4 half circles.

4 Spread the cream cheese frosting on top of 3 halves and stack the 4 halves, with the unfrosted half on top.

5 Turn cake over so it's resting on the sliced flat side with the curved side up, to form a half circle, or rainbow, shape.

6 Frost entire cake with cream cheese frosting. Then, with toothpick, lightly outline five half-rings on both sides of cake.

7 Using star-shaped tip, squirt blue frosting into center half-ring, green into the next ring, then yellow, then orange. Finish with red. Repeat for other side.

8 Attach candles along the top of the cake in a sunray design.

**VARIATIONS:** Instead of frosting the cake sides and leaving the top curve white, frost the top of the cake in the five rainbow colors, leaving the sides white. Tint the frosting yourself for a wider variety of colors.

**PRACTICAL TIP:** Use toothpicks to secure cake layers together after you turn them onto side.

# PATCHWORK CAKE

This Patchwork Cake makes a one-of-a-kind centerpiece the guests will be proud to make, serve—and eat!

- **Serves:** 10
- **Time:** 10 minutes to prepare
  30 minutes to bake
  1 hour to freeze (optional)
  20 minutes to decorate
- **Complexity:** Easy

## INGREDIENTS

- 1 package low-fat angel food, carrot, or favorite cake mix
- Vegetable spray
- 4 cans low-fat cream cheese frosting (or see page 211 for our recipe)
- Food coloring, any 4 colors
- Tubes of frosting with decorator tips

## MATERIALS

- Large rectangular baking pan
- Knife
- Plastic wrap
- 4 medium bowls
- Small decorative sprinkles, candies, fruit, toys, candles
- 10 plates
- Large serving platter

## WHAT TO DO

**1** Prepare the cake batter, pour into rectangular baking pan sprayed with vegetable spray, and bake according to package directions. Cool.

**2** Cut cake into slices, wrap each in plastic wrap, and freeze for 1 hour or more.

**3** Place equal parts of the cream cheese frosting into 4 bowls and tint each a different color.

**4** Set out bowls of frosting, tubes, decorations, and candles. Distribute plates and frozen cake slices, unwrapped, to guests at the table.

**5** Have the guests frost their individual cake slices with cream cheese frosting and decorate the slices using tubes, sprinkles, candies, fruit, and toys.

**6** When everyone is finished, assemble the individual slices on a serving platter into one large Patchwork Cake and set on the table as a centerpiece to admire. Then let the guests eat their own decorated slices.

**VARIATIONS:** Ahead of time, spell out a message or the name of the birthday child, 1 letter per piece of paper. Distribute the letters and have each guest write that letter as part of the design on his or her slice. When all have finished, place slices together to spell out the message or name.

**PRACTICAL TIP:** Freezing the cake ahead of time is not necessary, but the slightly frozen cake is firmer and so will be easier to frost.

# PLAY BALL! CAKE

Watch the team spirit for all kinds of sports come alive with our Play Ball! Cake.

- **Serves:** 12
- **Time:** 10 minutes to prepare
  30 minutes to bake
  20 minutes to decorate
- **Complexity:** Easy

## INGREDIENTS

- 1 package low-fat carrot cake or angel food cake mix
- 2 cans low-fat cream cheese frosting (or see page 211 for our recipe)
- 2 cups coconut, shredded
- Food coloring, green
- Tubes of frosting with decorator tips

## MATERIALS

- Rectangular or square cake pan
- Cardboard the size of the cake pan, wrapped with aluminum foil
- Plastic bag
- Small plastic sports figures or other sports-related accessories and decorative candies

## WHAT TO DO

1 Prepare cake batter, pour into cake pan, bake cake according to package directions, and turn out onto cardboard.

2 Spread frosting over cake.

3 Put coconut into a plastic bag, add several drops of green food coloring, and shake until coconut is evenly coated.

4 Sprinkle coconut over cake to make grass.

5 Use frosting tubes to make football field, soccer field, basketball court, or baseball diamond.

6 Make grids, goal posts, bases, hoops, and so on using candies.

7 Add plastic sports figures and set up a game.

**VARIATIONS:** You can use a rectangular cake to make lots of creative cakes, such as a shirt, a pair of shorts or pants, a ticket, a credit card, a certificate, a picture frame, a box of chocolates, an envelope, and so on.

**PRACTICAL TIPS:** Cut the rectangular cake into other shapes to create what you want, such as a diamond, a square, a star, a puzzle piece, and so on.

# RIBBON CAKE

These colorful ribbons are revealed when the cake is cut.

- **Serves:** 12
- **Time:** 10 minutes to prepare
  45 to 50 minutes to bake
  2 hours to refrigerate
- **Complexity:** Easy

## INGREDIENTS

- 1 package low-fat white or yellow cake mix
- 1 3-ounce package sugar-free instant vanilla pudding
- 4 eggs
- ¼ cup oil
- Vegetable spray
- 1 3-ounce package sugar-free raspberry gelatin
- 3 cups water, 2 cold and 1 boiling
- Sugar-free whipped topping

## MATERIALS

- Large mixing bowl
- Mixer
- 13-by-9-inch baking pan
- Toothpick

## WHAT TO DO

**1** Preheat oven to 350 degrees.

**2** Combine cake mix with pudding, eggs, 1 cup cold water, and oil in mixing bowl; beat until smooth.

**3** Pour into pan sprayed with vegetable spray and bake at 350 degrees for 45 to 50 minutes.

**4** While cake cools, dissolve gelatin in 1 cup boiling water. Then add 1 cup cold water.

**5** Poke holes all over warm cake with toothpick, about ½ inch apart, and pour gelatin mixture over cake.

**6** Chill 2 hours or more in refrigerator.

**7** Top with sugar-free whipped topping and cut.

**VARIATIONS:** Use any flavor of gelatin. Frost cake.

**PRACTICAL TIP:** Pour gelatin over cake while the cake is still warm for best results.

# SUNKEN TREASURE CAKE

Sunken Treasure Cake makes a big splash at any type of beach bash, pirate party, or Hawaiian luau. When the cake is gone, your guests can take home the leftover loot!

- **Serves:** 10 to 12
- **Time:** 10 minutes to prepare
  30 minutes to bake
  20 minutes to decorate
- **Complexity:** Easy

## INGREDIENTS

- 1 package low-fat angel food, chiffon, or carrot cake mix
- 2 cans low-fat cream cheese frosting (or see page 211 for our recipe)
- 2 tablespoons cocoa
- Frosting tubes with decorator tips
- Chocolate gold coins
- Assorted small candies

## MATERIALS

- Sheet-cake pan
- Cardbord the size of the cake pan, wrapped with aluminum foil
- Fake jewelry or necklaces made from cereal, macaroni, or Life Savers

## WHAT TO DO

**1** Prepare cake according to package direction, pour into the sheet-cake pan, and bake.

**2** Combine softened cream cheese frosting and cocoa.

**3** When cake is cool, turn it onto foil-covered cardboard and frost with chocolate-flavored frosting.

**4** Clean the sheet-cake pan and frost it too, inside and out.

**5** Set the pan at right angles to the cake so it looks like an open treasure chest.

**6** Decorate the cake and pan with tubes of frosting, chocolate gold coins, assorted candies, and fake or candy jewelry.

**VARIATION:** Make the cake look like an open present with a gift inside.

**PRACTICAL TIP:** Slip cake just under lip of cake pan to secure pan and keep it from falling over under the weight of decorations.

# VOLCANIC MOON CAKE

Take the cake back to the prehistoric past, or forward to the futuristic frontier, to suit your party theme. This cake will "rock" the place!

- **Serves:** 12
- **Time:** 20 minutes to prepare
  30 minutes to bake
  15 minutes to decorate
- **Complexity:** Moderate

## INGREDIENTS

- 1 package low-fat chiffon or angel food cake mix
- Vegetable spray
- ½ cup sugar
- ⅛ cup coffee, decaffeinated
- ⅛ cup corn syrup
- 1 teaspoon baking soda
- 1 cup heavy cream
- 1 tablespoon sugar
- 1 teaspoon vanilla

## MATERIALS

- Sheet-cake pan
- Large saucepan, at least 5 inches deep
- Candy thermometer
- Spoon
- 8-by-10-inch shallow metal pan
- Mixer

## WHAT TO DO

1 Prepare cake mix according to package directions, pour into sheet-cake pan sprayed with vegetable spray, bake, and cool.

2 Mix sugar, coffee, and corn syrup in saucepan. Bring to a boil and cook to hard-crack stage (310 degrees).

3 Remove from heat and immediately add baking soda.

4 Stir until mixture thickens and pulls from the sides; don't overbeat.

5 Pour foam into ungreased shallow pan, but do not spread; let stand until cool.

6 Knock out hardened foam from pan and break into chunks.

7 Whip cream with sugar and vanilla. Then remove cake from pan, spread whipped cream over cake, and cover cake with crushed topping.

8 Refrigerate until party time.

**VARIATIONS:** Add dinosaurs to the top of the cake to give it a Jurassic Park look. Or make it a moon cake and set small astronauts on top.

**PRACTICAL TIP:** Use a small kitchen hammer to break up foam.

# ICE-CREAM DREAMS

We all scream for ice cream, but the ice cream doesn't have to be high in sugar and fat. Creative ice-cream desserts are easy to make, using delicious substitutions. You can serve a pastel sherbet or an icy sorbet, or work your party magic with low-fat or nonfat frozen yogurt. The ice-cream section of the store has brands of ice cream that feature reduced sugar and fat.

Use your imagination when serving your ice-cream desserts and make the ice cream part of the party fun. To make your ice-cream dreams come true, serve ice cream instead of cake, make ice-cream-and-cake combination desserts, or try one of our unique recipes.

# AVALANCHE!

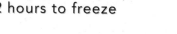

Here's a mountain of cake and ice cream buried under an avalanche of whipped cream!

- **Serves:** 8
- **Time:** 20 minutes to prepare
  2 hours to freeze
- **Complexity:** Easy

## INGREDIENTS

- 8 low-fat muffins, any flavor
- ½ cup low-sugar strawberry jam
- 1 quart low-fat frozen yogurt, any flavor
- 1 large container nondairy whipped topping

## MATERIALS

- 8 dessert plates
- Knife
- Ice-cream scoop or spoon

## WHAT TO DO

**1** Place muffins on dessert plates and slice off rounded tops.

**2** Spread strawberry jam on tops of muffins.

**3** Place one large rounded scoop of frozen yogurt on top of jam.

**4** Replace tops of muffins.

**5** Place muffins in freezer for 2 hours.

**6** At serving time, cover each muffin completely with whipped topping.

**VARIATIONS:** Cover the muffins with cream cheese frosting or meringue instead of whipped topping.

**PRACTICAL TIP:** Freeze muffins completely before adding whipped topping for easier serving.

# CAKE-'N'-ICE-CREAM SANDWICHES

This Cake-'n'-Ice-Cream Sandwich is portable, fun to eat, and unique!

- **Serves:** 8
- **Time:** 20 minutes to prepare
  1 hour to freeze
- **Complexity:** Easy

## INGREDIENTS

- 16 small angel food dessert cakes or 8 cupcakes or muffins
- ½ gallon favorite flavor low-fat frozen yogurt, softened

## MATERIALS

- Pastry bag (optional)
- Knife
- Aluminum foil or plastic wrap

## WHAT TO DO

**1** If you're using cupcakes or muffins, cut them in half to make two sandwich parts.

**2** Fill pastry bag with softened frozen yogurt, or just use a knife, and spread yogurt on 8 dessert cakes or bottom halves of cupcakes or muffins.

**3** Top with dessert cake, cupcake top, or muffin top to make Cake-'n'-Ice-Cream Sandwich.

**4** Wrap each sandwich in foil or plastic wrap and freeze until serving time.

**VARIATIONS:** Use large soft cookies, such as oatmeal, chocolate chip, or peanut butter, instead of dessert cakes, to make sandwiches.

**PRACTICAL TIP:** Pipe ice cream with pastry bag into spirals for easy filling.

# ROLL AND FREEZE ICE CREAM

Campers use this method to create their own ice cream treat. Let everyone have a turn to roll and freeze the ice-cream cans!

- **Serves:** 2 to 3
- **Time:** 10 minutes to roll
  20 minutes to freeze
- **Complexity:** Easy

## INGREDIENTS

- 1 cup heavy cream
- 1 cup nonfat milk
- 1 beaten egg
- ⅓ cup sugar
- 1 teaspoon vanilla

## MATERIALS

- 2 coffee cans, one larger than the other, with lids, per 2 guests
- Crushed ice
- Rock salt

## WHAT TO DO

1. Collect several large and small coffee cans, depending on how many containers you want to make.

2. Combine cream, milk, egg, sugar, and vanilla in the smaller coffee can and close the can with a lid.

3. Set smaller can in larger can, fill space between them with layers of crushed ice and rock salt, and close the larger can with a lid.

4. Have two kids sit across from each other, legs apart, and tell them to roll the can back and forth between each other for 10 minutes.

5. Open larger can and remove water, salt, and ice. Stir contents of inner can and replace the lid.

6. Fill space again with layers of crushed ice and rock salt, replace the lids, and roll another 5 to 10 minutes.

7. Remove smaller can and scoop out ice cream.

**VARIATIONS:** For a variety of flavors, add fruit, such as strawberry puree, to the ice cream.

**PRACTICAL TIP:** Have the kids play word games or sing songs while they roll the cans back and forth, to help pass the time.

# CHOCOLATE-LACE PIE

The lacy chocolate covering on this ice-cream pie will fascinate your guests.

- **Serves:** 10
- **Time:** 30 minutes to prepare
  2 hours to freeze
- **Complexity:** Moderate

## INGREDIENTS

- 1 chocolate cookie or graham cracker pie crust, store-bought or homemade (see page 211 for our recipe)
- 1 quart favorite low-fat frozen yogurt, softened
- Vegetable spray
- 12 ounces semisweet chocolate pieces or baking squares
- 1 to 2 tablespoons nonfat milk

## MATERIALS

- Large bowl the diameter of the pie pan
- Microwave or stove
- Microwave-safe bowl or double boiler
- Spoon

## WHAT TO DO

**1** Spread softened yogurt in pie crust; place in freezer for 1 hour or more.

**2** Turn bowl upside down and spray vegetable spray around the outside bottom and sides.

**3** Heat chocolate and milk in double boiler or microwave, until mixture is smooth.

**4** Remove from heat and cool slightly.

**5** Drizzle hot chocolate from the tip of a spoon over the flipped bowl to create a swirled, open-web pattern.

**6** Allow chocolate to cool on counter until it becomes firm. Then carefully loosen from bowl but do not remove it.

**7** Place chocolate-covered bowl in refrigerator to chill and firm up.

**8** At serving time, remove ice-cream pie from freezer and chocolate-covered bowl from refrigerator.

**9** Carefully remove chocolate web and place on top of ice-cream pie. Serve immediately.

**VARIATIONS:** Use two flavors of frozen yogurt. Top the pie with white chocolate instead of semisweet chocolate.

**PRACTICAL TIP:** Spray the bowl generously to keep chocolate from sticking.

# CHOCOLATE NOODLES

Whoever heard of Chocolate Noodles for an ice cream treat? Your guests will get a kick out of this new twist to an old favorite.

- **Serves:** 10
- **Time:** 30 minutes to prepare
  30 minutes to bake
- **Complexity:** Easy

## INGREDIENTS

- 1 package low-fat, low-sugar brownie mix
- 1 12-ounce package chocolate or carob chips
- 2 tablespoons light corn syrup
- 2 tablespoons low-fat margarine
- Vegetable spray
- ½ low-fat frozen yogurt, any flavor
- White chocolate shavings (optional)

## MATERIALS

- Heavy saucepan
- Wax paper
- Rolling pin
- Long, sharp knife; pizza cutter; or rimless cookie sheet
- Ice-cream scoop or spoon
- 10 dessert plates

## WHAT TO DO

**1** Bake brownies according to package directions, cool, and cut into squares—1 for each guest.

**2** Melt chips, syrup, and margarine in heavy saucepan over low heat.

**3** Lay wax paper on a flat surface and lightly spray with vegetable spray.

**4** Spoon 4 tablespoons of the chocolate mixture onto the wax paper and top with more wax paper sprayed with vegetable spray.

**5** Roll chocolate to ⅛-inch thickness.

# Ice Cream Dreams

**6** Remove top layer of waxed paper and allow the rolled chocolate to cool and set while you prepare rest of the liquid chocolate the same way.

**7** With a knife, pizza cutter, or edge of a rimless cookie sheet, slice the chocolate sheet into thin strips to form "noodles."

**8** Place brownies on dessert plates and top with scoop of frozen yogurt.

**9** Lift wax paper and "pour" equal amount of chocolate strips onto each scoop of frozen yogurt, making a loose coil as you go.

**10** Top with shredded white chocolate for "Parmesan cheese."

**VARIATION:** Use white chocolate and tint it different colors.

**PRACTICAL TIPS:** Handle chocolate strips carefully—they melt quickly in your hands. Cool in refrigerator a few minutes if necessary.

# CHERRY CHILL

This extra-fruity dessert is deliciously different.

- **Serves:** 10
- **Time:** 20 minutes to prepare
  2 hours to freeze
- **Complexity:** Easy

## INGREDIENTS

- 2 16-ounce cans cherries, light or dark
- 1 8-ounce can crushed pineapple
- 1 pint vanilla low-fat frozen yogurt, softened
- ½ cup chocolate syrup
- 2 tablespoons lemon juice
- ⅛ cup chopped nuts, coconut, or granola
- 2 cups low-fat, low-sugar whipped topping (optional)
- 1 6-ounce bag miniature chocolate chips (optional)

## MATERIALS

- Knife
- Spoon
- 8-inch square pan
- Aluminum foil

## WHAT TO DO

**1** Drain cherries and pineapple.

**2** Chop cherries.

**3** Combine fruits with frozen yogurt, chocolate syrup, and lemon juice.

**4** Turn mixture into square pan and cover with foil.

**5** Freeze until firm.

**6** Remove from freezer and let stand at room temperature for 30 minutes.

**7** Cut into squares, and top with nuts, coconut, or granola; whipped topping; and chocolate chips, if desired.

**VARIATIONS:** Choose a fruit-flavored frozen yogurt for an extra-fruity taste. Add mandarin orange slices, kiwi slices, or chopped grapes. Instead of topping the dessert with chocolate chips, make chocolate curls using a semisweet chocolate bar.

**PRACTICAL TIP:** Spray the pan with vegetable spray before filling it with the yogurt mixture so the yogurt mixture can be easily removed.

# CHOCOLATE MARSHMALLOW

Please your guests with the soft, sweet taste of homemade chocolate marshmallow "ice cream."

- **Serves:** 8
- **Time:** 20 minutes to prepare
  2 hours to freeze
- **Complexity:** Easy

## INGREDIENTS
- 2 8-ounce jars marshmallow cream
- 1⅓ cups unsweetened cocoa powder
- 6 cups low-fat milk

## MATERIALS
- Large, heavy saucepan
- Square or rectangular pan, any size
- Spoon (for stirring)
- 8 dessert dishes

## WHAT TO DO

1. Mix marshmallow cream and cocoa together in saucepan over medium heat, stirring until melted and smooth.

2. Remove from heat, add milk, and stir until blended.

3. Pour into pan and freeze for ½ hour.

4. Remove from freezer, stir, smooth, and refreeze for another ½ hour.

5. Repeat step 4 and freeze for another hour.

6. Serve in dessert dishes.

**VARIATIONS:** Top with nondairy whipped topping. Or pour mixture into ice-cream maker and follow directions for making ice cream.

**PRACTICAL TIP:** Stirring the frozen mixture from time to time keeps it well blended, fluffy, and light.

# MAKE-A-FACE CLOWN CONES

Let your guests use their imagination to create a one-of-a-kind clown. They're fun to make and fun to eat—and each one is unique!

- **Serves:** 8
- **Time:** 30 minutes to prepare
  2 hours to freeze
- **Complexity:** Easy

## INGREDIENTS

- 8 large cookies, such as oatmeal, chocolate chip, or peanut butter
- 1 quart low-fat frozen yogurt, any flavor
- 8 ice-cream cones, pointed
- Tubes of frosting with decorator tips
- Small candy or dried fruit for decorations
- Spray can of low-fat whipping cream

## MATERIALS

- 8 dessert plates
- Large spoon or ice cream scoop

## WHAT TO DO

**1** Place large cookies on individual plates.

**2** Scoop a ball of frozen yogurt onto each cookie.

**3** Place a cone upside down on top of each yogurt ball to make clown hat.

**4** Freeze the cones until firm, about 2 hours.

**5** Set out decorations and tubes of frosting. Give each guest a clown cone. Have them create their own clowns with the supplies provided.

**6** Squirt the top of the cone with a fluffy ball of whipped cream.

**7** Serve immediately.

**VARIATIONS:** Instead of clowns, make monsters, funny-looking people, or animals, using your imagination.

**PRACTICAL TIPS:** Tell your guests to work quickly before their clowns melt! Prepare the cones before the party (maybe even the day before), and then simply take them out of the freezer for your guests to decorate when dessert time arrives.

# ICE-CREAM-'N'-CANDY PIE

Put the kids' two favorite treats together and you get an Ice-Cream-'n'-Candy Pie. You can be creative with this one, and make the guest of honor's favorite flavors all in one delicious dessert!

- **Serves:** 10
- **Time:** 20 minutes to prepare
  2 hours to freeze
- **Complexity:** Easy

## INGREDIENTS

- 1 chocolate cookie pie crust, store-bought or homemade (see page 211 for our recipe)
- 2 1-pint containers of favorite flavors low-fat frozen yogurts, softened
- ½ cup favorite candies, chopped or crushed, sugar-free if preferred
- 1 large container low-fat whipped cream
- 3 tablespoons multicolored candy sprinkles

## MATERIALS

- Pie pan
- Knife
- 10 dessert dishes

## WHAT TO DO

**1** Spread 1 flavor of softened frozen yogurt in pie crust, filling half full. Smooth yogurt with a knife.

**2** Sprinkle half the candies on top of yogurt.

**3** Place in freezer for about 1 hour.

**4** Remove pie and spread second flavor of softened yogurt on top, creating a mound.

**5** Sprinkle remaining candies on top.

**6** Return to freezer for another hour or more.

**7** At serving time, top with whipped cream and sprinkle multicolored candies on top.

**VARIATIONS:** Use any two compatible flavors of frozen yogurt you like. Go crazy with a third flavor!

**PRACTICAL TIPS:** Soften the first pint of yogurt before beginning pie. Remove the second flavor of yogurt from the freezer shortly before adding it to the first layer.

# EGGS IN THE NEST

This unique ice cream dish is perfect for the nature, science, or animal party!

- **Serves:** 8
- **Time:** 15 minutes preparation
  30 minutes to refrigerate
- **Complexity:** Easy

## INGREDIENTS

- 1 12-ounce package chocolate or carob chips
- 1 tablespoon low-fat margarine
- 2 cups canned chow mien noodles or shredded-wheat cereal, crushed
- 1 cup unsalted peanuts, chopped
- ½ gallon low-fat frozen yogurt, any flavor (vanilla is most egglike)

## MATERIALS

- Medium heavy saucepan or microwave bowl
- Stove or microwave
- Wax paper
- Spoon
- 8 dessert plates

## WHAT TO DO

**1** Melt chocolate with margarine in microwave or over low heat in saucepan.

**2** Stir in noodles or crushed shredded wheat and chopped peanuts.

**3** Make 8 mounds of mixture on wax paper and indent middle with a spoon to form nest.

**4** Refrigerate for 30 minutes.

**5** When firm, fill each nest with small, rounded scoops of frozen yogurt to form eggs.

**VARIATION:** Substitute 2 cups peanut butter or 2 cups marshmallows for chocolate chips.

**PRACTICAL TIPS:** Add a little milk to chocolate chips if they don't melt smoothly. Let the mixture cool a few minutes before making mounds on wax paper so the nests hold up better.

# FLIP-OVER SUNDAE

**Y**our guests will flip over this Flip-Over Sundae when they realize it's upside down!

- **Serves:** 8
- **Time:** 20 minutes to prepare
  1 to 2 hours to freeze
- **Complexity:** Easy

## INGREDIENTS

- 8 maraschino cherries or purple seedless grapes
- ½ cup nuts, chopped
- ½ cup peanut butter
- ½ cup low-sugar strawberry jam
- 1 cup low-fat, sugar-free whipped topping
- ½ cup carob or chocolate syrup (optional)
- ½ gallon favorite flavor low-fat frozen yogurt, softened

## MATERIALS

- Microwave
- Microwave-safe bowl
- Teaspoon
- 8 dessert cups

## WHAT TO DO

1. Place cherries or grapes at the bottom of dessert cups.

2. Sprinkle equal amounts of chopped nuts over cherries or grapes.

3. Heat peanut butter in microwave until melted; drizzle over nuts.

4. Drop several teaspoons of jam over peanut butter.

5. Spread whipped topping over all.

6. Drizzle chocolate syrup over topping (optional).

7. Spread softened frozen yogurt over all the ingredients and smooth the top, reaching all sides of the dessert cup to seal.

8. Place in freezer for 1 to 2 hours to refreeze.

**VARIATIONS:** Make your own favorite sundae recipes but in reverse! Add bananas for a banana split, two flavors of frozen yogurt, or other toppings.

**PRACTICAL TIP:** Use transparent dessert cups so your guests can see through the glass (or plastic). If you don't have transparent cups, your guests will still have fun discovering the surprise inside these Flip-Over Sundaes.

# BLOOMING CUPCAKES

The kids will love this creepy crawly ice-cream dish. Why? Because it's gross!

- **Serves:** 12
- **Time:** 20 minutes to prepare
  20 minutes to bake
  2 hours to freeze
- **Complexity:** Easy

## INGREDIENTS

- 1 package chocolate or carrot cake mix or favorite recipe
- ½ gallon carton of low-fat chocolate frozen yogurt, softened
- 1 box chocolate wafer cookies or low-fat, low-sugar graham crackers, crushed to a fine powder
- Gummy Worms

## MATERIALS

- Cupcake tin
- 12 cupcake liners
- Spoon
- 12 small plastic flowers with stems

## WHAT TO DO

**1** Prepare cake mix according to package directions. Line cupcake tin with cupcake liners, and fill half full with batter.

**2** Bake according to package directions, remove from cupcake tin, and cool completely.

**3** Top each cupcake with a spoonful of softened chocolate frozen yogurt.

**4** Sprinkle crushed cookies over yogurt to make "dirt."

**5** Insert Gummy Worms into cupcake, half in, half hanging over the side.

**6** Stick small plastic flowers into the center of each mound of yogurt.

**7** Freeze until serving time.

**VARIATIONS:** Add any Gummy bugs and other critters you can find in the candy department for added fun. Bury some of the Gummy Worms under the frozen yogurt to be discovered as the kids dig in.

**PRACTICAL TIPS:** Remove flowers when placing cupcakes in freezer, and reinsert at serving time. To save time, crush cookies or crackers while yogurt softens.

# FROZEN OAT BARS

**Y**our guests will love to bite into these homemade, crunchy, chewy, yummy oat bars (which are low in sugar and high in good nutrition).

- **Serves:** 12
- **Time:** 20 minutes to prepare
  20 minutes to bake
  2 hours to freeze
- **Complexity:** Easy

## INGREDIENTS

- 1 cup flour
- ¼ cup regular oats, uncooked
- ½ cup nuts, chopped
- ¼ cup brown sugar, firmly packed
- ½ cup low-fat butter, softened
- 1 cup butterscotch topping
- 1 quart vanilla low-fat frozen yogurt, softened

## MATERIALS

- Large mixing bowl
- 2 knives
- Spoon
- Jelly-roll pan
- 8-inch square baking pan
- Plastic wrap or aluminum foil

## WHAT TO DO

**1** Preheat oven to 350 degrees.

**2** Combine flour, oats, nuts, and brown sugar in bowl. Cut in soft butter with 2 knives until crumbly.

**3** Spread the oat mixture in the jelly-roll pan and bake 20 minutes at 350 degrees, stirring occasionally, until lightly browned. Remove from oven; cool.

**4** Spread half the mixture in bottom of square baking pan.

**5** Spoon ½ cup butterscotch topping over top of oat mixture, spread softened frozen yogurt over sauce, spoon the rest of the butterscotch topping over the frozen yogurt, and top with remaining oat mixture.

**6** Cover with plastic wrap or aluminum foil and freeze until firm, about 2 hours.

**7** Cut into bars and serve.

**VARIATION:** Mix oat mixture with softened yogurt in a bowl and freeze. Serve chunky-style frozen dessert in individual dessert dishes.

**PRACTICAL TIP:** You can make the bars a day before the party, wrap each bar individually, and freeze until serving time.

# FRUITY POPS

Here's a colorful, different, and delicious dessert on a stick.

- **Serves:** 8
- **Time:** 15 minutes to prepare
  2 hours to freeze
- **Complexity:** Easy

## INGREDIENTS

- 1 12-ounce can frozen orange juice or lemonade concentrate
- 1 large can fruit cocktail

## MATERIALS

- Large pitcher
- Spoon
- 8 ice-cream molds or ice cube tray with 8 ice-cream sticks

## WHAT TO DO

**1** Mix orange juice or lemonade in pitcher according to package directions.

**2** Stir in fruit cocktail.

**3** Pour into ice cream molds or ice cube trays and add ice cream sticks.

**4** Place in freezer until firm, about 2 hours.

**5** When pops are frozen, pop out and serve to guests.

**VARIATIONS:** Use large package of Jell-O instead of juice concentrate. Add cut-up fruit instead of fruit cocktail.

**PRACTICAL TIP:** Be sure Fruity Pops are fully frozen before serving.

# ICE-CREAM PIZZA

Combine the kids' favorites—ice cream and pizza—into one delicious dessert!

- **Serves:** 10
- **Time:** 20 minutes to prepare
  25 to 30 minutes to bake
- **Complexity:** Easy

## INGREDIENTS

- 2 20-ounce packages refrigerator cookie dough, such as sugar, chocolate chip, oatmeal, or chocolate
- Vegetable spray
- 1 quart favorite flavor low-fat frozen yogurt, softened
- 1 cup low-sugar strawberry jam
- Decorative toppings, such as sprinkles, small candies, dried fruits, seeds, or chopped nuts

## MATERIALS

- 16-inch pizza pan
- 10 dessert plates

## WHAT TO DO

**1** Preheat oven to 350 degrees.

**2** Press refrigerator dough onto pizza pan sprayed with vegetable spray.

**3** Bake at 350 degrees for 25 to 30 minutes, until lightly browned; cool.

**4** Spread softened frozen yogurt over crust.

**5** Add a layer of strawberry jam.

**6** Top with decorative toppings.

**7** Cut into wedges and serve.

**VARIATIONS:** Use fruit, such as sliced kiwis, sliced strawberries, whole blueberries, and so on, to decorate the pizza in a fancy pattern.

**PRACTICAL TIP:** Prepare the pizza hours before the party and freeze until serving time.

# PINK CLOUD

**A** light and fluffy dessert to serve with or without cake.

- **Serves:** 10
- **Time:** 20 minutes to prepare
  1 hour to freeze
  2 to 3 minutes to broil
- **Complexity:** Moderate

## INGREDIENTS

- 10 angel food dessert cakes
- ½ gallon low-fat raspberry sherbet
- 6 egg whites
- 2 teaspoons vanilla
- ½ teaspoon cream of tartar
- Food coloring, red
- ½ cup sugar

## MATERIALS

- 10 oven-proof dessert plates
- Large spoon or ice cream scoop
- Large mixing bowl
- Mixer

## WHAT TO DO

**1** Place dessert cakes on individual plates.

**2** Top with large, rounded scoop of raspberry sherbet.

**3** Freeze until serving time.

**4** In large bowl, mix egg whites, vanilla, and cream of tartar, and beat at high speed until frothy.

**5** Add a few drops of red food coloring to tint meringue pink.

**6** Gradually add sugar and beat until stiff peaks form.

**7** Remove desserts from freezer and completely cover with meringue.

**8** Broil 6 inches away from heat until lightly browned, 2 or 3 minutes.

**VARIATIONS:** Use other flavors of sherbet and tint the meringue to match.

**PRACTICAL TIP:** Make sure sherbet is frozen before topping with meringue.

# SPAGHETTI ICE CREAM

A dessert that looks just like a spaghetti dinner—but tastes like an ice-cream dessert!

- **Serves:** 8
- **Time:** 30 minutes to prepare
  1 hour to freeze
- **Complexity:** Moderate

## INGREDIENTS

- 1 quart low-fat frozen vanilla yogurt
- 1 cup low-sugar strawberry or raspberry jam
- ½ cup white chocolate, grated

## MATERIALS

- Potato ricer, meat grinder, cheese grater, pasta maker, or other "noodle" press
- 8 dinner plates
- Plastic wrap
- Spoon

## WHAT TO DO

**1** Push ⅛-inch-thick slice of frozen yogurt through ricer, grinder, grater or other press onto each dinner plate, to make noodles.

**2** As you fill each plate with "spaghetti," wrap each plate gently in plastic wrap and immediately place in freezer.

**3** At serving time, top plates of "spaghetti" with spoonfuls of jam for "sauce" and grated white chocolate for "cheese."

**VARIATION:** Sprinkle with coconut instead of white chocolate for cheese.

**PRACTICAL TIP:** Work quickly to prevent frozen yogurt from melting and losing its spaghetti shape.

# SUNSET PARFAIT

**R**ibbons of color make this ice-cream dish a special addition to your party refreshments.

- **Serves:** 8
- **Time:** 20 minutes to prepare 2 hours to freeze
- **Complexity:** Easy

## INGREDIENTS

- ½ gallon vanilla low-fat frozen yogurt, softened
- Food coloring, yellow, orange, red, purple, and blue
- Low-fat or nondairy whipped cream

## MATERIALS

- Ice-cream scoop or spoon
- 5 medium-sized bowls
- 8 parfait or other tall transparent glasses

## WHAT TO DO

**1** Spoon an equal portion of frozen yogurt into each of 5 bowls.

**2** Tint each serving of yogurt a different color with food coloring.

**3** Layer the colors in the parfait glasses, beginning with yellow, then orange, red, purple, and blue (last), to make "sunset."

**4** Serve with a cloud of whipped cream on top.

**VARIATIONS:** Tint the frozen yogurt any colors you like and layer them into the parfait glasses. Substitute sugar-free vanilla pudding for frozen yogurt.

**PRACTICAL TIPS:** To make purple, combine red and blue food coloring. To make orange, combine red and yellow food coloring. To prevent breakage, use plastic parfait glasses instead of glass.

# SUNSHINE SNOWBALLS

Capture sunshine in a snowball and serve it to your special guests. You can be creative with the fillings and with interesting containers, so use this recipe as a starting point for other Sunshine Snowballs!

- **Serves:** Serves 8
- **Time:** 20 minutes to prepare
  2 hours to freeze
- **Complexity:** Easy

## INGREDIENTS

- 8 oranges, grapefruit, coconuts, cantaloupes, or papayas
- ½ gallon matching fruit sherbet or low-fat frozen yogurt, softened

## MATERIALS

- Ice-cream scoop or spoon
- Tubes of frostings with fine-point tip

## WHAT TO DO

**1** Cut the tops off the fruit and set tops aside.

**2** Scoop out the pulp and drain the liquid.

**3** Fill the empty shells with sherbet or frozen yogurt.

**4** Replace the tops.

**5** Draw designs, happy faces, names, or other images on the outsides of the shells, using tubes of colorful frosting.

**6** Place filled shells in freezer until firm, about 2 hours.

**7** Soften on the counter for a few minutes before serving.

**VARIATIONS:** Cut a watermelon in half and scoop out fruit. Fill with raspberry sherbet, smooth top to make it look like a watermelon half, and dot with chocolate chips to make seeds.

**PRACTICAL TIPS:** Dry off outside of shells before frosting, so decorations will stick. To make extra-fruity snowballs, combine the fruit pulp and juice with the sherbet or frozen yogurt before filling the shells; if you want to hide the fruit, blend the yogurt and the pulp in a blender until smooth.

# RING AROUND THE ROSY

This tricky-looking sherbet dessert is easy to make, fun to look at, and delicious to eat.

- **Serves:** 12
- **Time:** 30 minutes to prepare
  2 hours or more to freeze
- **Complexity:** Easy

## INGREDIENTS

- 1 pint orange sherbet, softened
- 1 pint strawberry or raspberry sherbet, softened
- 1 pint coconut sherbet, softened
- 1 pint lime sherbet, softened

## MATERIALS

- Tube pan
- Spoon (for spreading)
- Serving platter
- 12 dessert plates

## WHAT TO DO

**1** Spread softened orange sherbet around the bottom of tube pan; smooth surface. Freeze for ½ hour or more.

**2** Remove from freezer. Scoop balls of strawberry or raspberry sherbet on top of orange sherbet without smoothing, and refreeze.

**3** Remove from freezer. Spread softened coconut sherbet around strawberry or raspberry sherbet; smooth surface. Refreeze.

**4** Remove from freezer. Spread softened lime sherbet on top of other layers; smooth surface. Refreeze.

**5** At serving time, remove sherbet from tube pan and place on platter.

**6** Slice and serve the colorful, surprising dessert to guests on individual dessert plates.

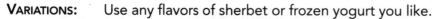

**VARIATIONS:** Use any flavors of sherbet or frozen yogurt you like.

**PRACTICAL TIP:** Spray pan with vegetable spray before filling with sherbet, or lightly run water around outside of pan to loosen sherbet.

# DynamIte Desserts

Party refreshments don't always have to be the traditional cake and ice cream. Some kids don't like cake and would prefer something different. For variety, you can offer your guests a fun and fancy dessert and tie it into your party's theme. Whether you create your own dessert or use the fun recipes in this chapter, begin with the basics kids love—Jell-O, pudding, ice cream, cookies, and so on—but make them more nutritious by choosing products low in fat and sugar, and high in vitamins, minerals, and fiber.

The following recipes are favorites among the younger crowd because these recipes use ingredients kids enjoy. We've added a unique twist to each dessert, but feel free to use your imagination and create your own new concoction!

# BANANA PEANUT BUTTER CHEESECAKE

Combine the kids' two favorite flavors into this rich and healthy dessert.

- **Serves:** 10
- **Time:** 20 minutes to prepare 40 minutes to bake
- **Complexity:** Easy

## INGREDIENTS

- Graham cracker crust, homemade or store-bought (see page 211 for our recipe)
- ½ cup chocolate or carob chips
- 8 ounces low-fat cream cheese
- 8 ounces low-fat farmer cheese
- ½ cup low-fat creamed cottage cheese or ricotta cheese
- 3 tablespoons honey
- ½ cup ripe bananas, mashed
- ½ cup low-fat peanut butter
- 3 eggs
- ½ cup peanuts, chopped

## MATERIALS

- Heavy saucepan or microwave-safe bowl
- Stove or microwave oven
- Medium bowl
- Mixer

## WHAT TO DO

**1** Preheat oven to 350 degrees.

**2** Melt chocolate or carob chips in microwave or in saucepan over low heat, and spread over graham cracker crust.

**3** In medium bowl, combine cheeses, honey, bananas, and peanut butter.

**4** Add eggs to mixture, one at a time, beating well after adding each egg.

**5** Pour mixture over crust, sprinkle chopped peanuts on top, and bake at 350 degrees for about 40 minutes, until done.

**6** Refrigerate until serving time.

**VARIATIONS:** Top with whipped topping. Then sprinkle chopped nuts and tiny chocolate chips on top.

**PRACTICAL TIP:** Another way to melt the chocolate or carob chips is to sprinkle them onto the graham cracker crust, pop the crust in the oven, and heat for a few minutes. Once the chocolate melts, spread it with a knife to cover surface of crust.

# BURIED TREASURE

A secret is hidden in this ordinary-looking dessert. Will the kids discover the Buried Treasure? You bet they will—all they need is a spoon!

- **Serves:** 8
- **Time:** 20 minutes to prepare
  1 hour to chill
- **Complexity:** Easy

## INGREDIENTS

- 2 4-ounce packages sugar-free chocolate pudding mix
- 2 cups nondairy whipped topping
- 8 strawberries, cherries, or small pieces of other fruit
- 16 chocolate wafer cookies, crushed
- 8 chocolate gold coins

## MATERIALS

- Large saucepan
- 2 spoons
- 8 dessert cups, preferably transparent
- 8 dessert spoons

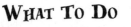

## WHAT TO DO

**1** Prepare pudding according to package directions and spoon mixture into dessert cups, filling halfway.

**2** Spread pudding on the bottom and up the sides of each cup, creating a small hole in the center.

**3** Spoon a small amount of whipped topping into the pudding hole, place a small piece of fruit in the whipped topping, and cover with more whipped topping.

**4** Cover the whipped topping with more chocolate pudding, filling the dessert cup. No whipped topping should show.

**5** Sprinkle the crushed chocolate wafer cookies over top of chocolate pudding.

**6** Set a chocolate gold coin on the top of the dessert for garnish. Then chill about 1 hour.

**7** Give the kids spoons and let them dig up the hidden treasure.

**VARIATIONS:** Tint the whipped topping a favorite color with food coloring. Use vanilla or other flavor of pudding. Add colorful candy sprinkles to whipped topping for an added surprise.

**PRACTICAL TIP:** If you use nontransparent dessert cups, you won't have to worry about the whipped topping showing through on the sides.

# CHOCOLATE QUICKSAND

Chocolate is delicious. Fruit is nutritious and delicious. When you combine them, you get a doubly delicious treat.

- **Serves:** 8
- **Time:** 30 minutes to prepare
- **Complexity:** Easy

## INGREDIENTS

- 2 12-ounce packages chocolate or carob chips
- ¼ cup low-fat margarine
- 2 tablespoons low-fat milk
- 2 cups strawberries
- 4 bananas, cut into chunks
- 2 peaches, cut into chunks
- 2 apples, cut into chunks
- 2 tangerines or oranges, peeled and separated
- 1 medium can pineapple chunks

## MATERIALS

- Heavy saucepan or microwave-safe bowl
- Stove or microwave
- 6 medium bowls (1 for each fruit)
- Large serving bowl
- 8 fondue forks, wooden skewers, or forks
- 8 dessert plates

## WHAT TO DO

**1** Slowly melt chocolate or carob with margarine and milk in saucepan over low heat, or in microwave-safe bowl in microwave.

**2** Place each type of fruit in a separate bowl on the table.

**3** When chocolate is melted, smooth, and blended, place in bowl in the center of the table (and tell the kids its hot).

**4** Give each guest a fondue fork and plate, and let them pick and choose which fruits they want to spear, dip, and eat.

**VARIATIONS:** Choose your favorite fruits and try them all! Use white chocolate instead of regular chocolate. Or just dip the fruit into yogurt.

**PRACTICAL TIPS:** When chocolate cools, it gets thick. Return to heat for a few minutes to soften again, or alternate two bowls of melted chocolate.

# COOKIES-'N'-CREAM CAKE

This tasty cheesecake has a delightful cookie crunch.

- **Serves:** 12
- **Time:** 20 minutes to prepare
  1 hour to bake
  1 hour (or more) to cool
- **Complexity:** Medium

## INGREDIENTS

- Vegetable spray
- 20 Oreo cookies
- 4 8-ounce packages low-fat cream cheese, softened
- 1 cup sugar
- 1½ teaspoons vanilla
- 2 teaspoons cornstarch
- 4 eggs
- ½ cup heavy cream

## MATERIALS

- 8-by-3-inch springform pan
- Large mixing bowl
- Mixer
- Spoon
- Large baking pan
- Serving platter

## WHAT TO DO

**1** Preheat oven to 350 degrees.

**2** Spray springform pan with vegetable spray and line bottom and sides with 12 cookies.

**3** Beat cream cheese in large bowl at medium speed until smooth.

**4** Beat in sugar, vanilla, and cornstarch. Add eggs one at a time, beating well after adding each egg. Then stir in heavy cream, mix, and spoon ⅓ mixture into cookie-lined pan.

**5** Crush remaining cookies. Sprinkle ⅓ of crumbs over mixture.

**6** Repeat, alternating cream cheese mixture and cookie crumbs, ending with cheese mixture.

**7** Set cake (in the springform pan) into large baking pan, place in oven, and add 1½ inches hot water to large pan.

**8** Bake at 350 degrees for 1 hour. When the cake is done, turn the oven off and leave the cake in the oven to cool for 1 hour.

**9** Remove cake from pan onto serving platter and cool on counter. Refrigerate until serving time.

**VARIATIONS:** Use peanut butter cookies, vanilla wafers, or other favorite cookies instead of Oreos.

**PRACTICAL TIP:** Wrap large pan in foil to prevent leakage.

# CRUNCHY COOKIE NECKLACE

A decorative necklace your guests can make, wear, and eat!

- **Serves:** 6
- **Time:** 30 minutes to prepare
  30 minutes to chill
  10 minutes to bake
  10 minutes to assemble
- **Complexity:** Easy

## INGREDIENTS

- Favorite sugar cookie recipe to make 4 dozen cookies (see page 209 for our recipe)
- Flour (for rolling dough)
- 4 tablespoons corn syrup
- 1 tablespoon water
- Food coloring, any colors
- Thin licorice whips

## MATERIALS

- Rolling pin
- Cookie cutters, any shapes
- Cookie sheet
- 1 large bowl
- 5 small bowls
- 6 paintbrushes

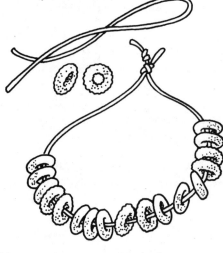

## WHAT TO DO

**1** Preheat the oven to 350 degrees.

**2** Divide cookie dough into thirds and flatten into 1-inch-thick rounds. Chill about 30 minutes.

**3** Roll out dough on floured surface to ¼-inch thickness and cut with cookie cutters into favorite shapes, 8 for each guest.

**4** Make a hole in center of each cookie and place on ungreased cookie sheet.

**5** Mix corn syrup and water, put an equal portion of the mixture into 5 small bowls, and tint with food coloring.

**6** Use paintbrushes to paint cookies with mixture.

**7** Put cookie sheet into oven and bake at 350 degrees for 8 to 10 minutes.

**8** When cool, thread licorice through holes to make an edible and wearable necklace.

**VARIATION:**  Instead of painting, color dough first with food coloring.

**PRACTICAL TIPS:** When it's time to roll the dough, have the guests work on pieces of foil lightly dusted with flour, to make transferring the dough to the cookie sheet easier.

# CREPE FRUZETTE

This fancy French fruit dessert is surprisingly easy to make.

- **Serves:** 10
- **Time:** 30 minutes to prepare
- **Complexity:** Easy

## INGREDIENTS

- 4 eggs
- 2 cups low-fat milk
- 2 cups flour
- ¼ teaspoon cinnamon
- Vegetable spray
- 1 cup blueberries
- 1 cup strawberries, sliced
- 1 cup mandarin orange slices
- 1 cup banana, sliced
- Whipped topping, low-fat fruit yogurt, or low-fat frozen yogurt

## MATERIALS

- 6-inch crepe pan or frying pan with nonstick surface
- 10 dessert plates

## WHAT TO DO

1. Beat eggs; combine with milk, flour, and cinnamon.

2. Heat crepe or frying pan sprayed with vegetable spray.

3. Pour just enough batter into pan to cover the bottom, and tilt pan in a circular motion to spread over surface.

4. Cook over medium heat a few minutes, until lightly browned. Turn and cook on other side until lightly browned.

5. Repeat with the rest of the batter to make 9 more crepes. Turn each cooked crepe onto its own plate.

6. Fill center of each crepe with a variety of fruits. Then fold each crepe like a burrito.

7. Serve with whipped topping, low-fat fruit yogurt, or low-fat frozen yogurt.

**VARIATIONS:** Instead of using fruit, fill the crepe with pudding, frozen yogurt, fruit yogurt, peanut butter and jelly, or other sweet fillings.

**PRACTICAL TIP:** Spray your nonstick pans with vegetable spray to be sure crepe comes off the pan easily.

# FRUIT PIZZA

Kids love fruit. Kids love pizza. And they'll go crazy for this fruity pizza!

- **Serves:** 12
- **Time:** 30 minutes to prepare
  15 minutes to bake
- **Complexity:** Easy

## INGREDIENTS

- 1 10-ounce package refrigerator sugar-cookie dough
- 2 8-ounce packages low-fat cream cheese, softened
- ¼ cup sugar
- ½ teaspoon vanilla
- 3 kiwis, thinly sliced
- 10 strawberries, thinly sliced
- 1 4-ounce can mandarin orange slices (reserve the juice)
- 2½ tablespoons cornstarch
- ½ cup cold water
- 1 cup orange juice (including mandarin orange juice)
- ¼ cup lemon juice
- ¾ cup sugar

## MATERIALS

- 12-inch round pizza pan
- Medium bowl
- Saucepan
- Pizza cutter
- 12 dessert plates

## WHAT TO DO

**1** Slice dough into thin rounds, place on pizza pan, and press to fill pan evenly.

**2** Bake according to package directions, until lightly browned. Cool.

**3** Mix cream cheese, sugar, and vanilla together in a medium bowl.

**4** Spread mixture on cooled cookie and top with fruit in a fancy circular design.

**5** Dissolve cornstarch in cold water, add remaining ingredients, and heat in saucepan over low heat. Cool.

**6** Pour mixture evenly over the fruit and cookie.

**7** At serving time, cut into wedges and serve on dessert plates.

**VARIATIONS:** Choose your favorite fruits to decorate the pizza.

**PRACTICAL TIP:** Pinch up the edge of the cookie dough to keep liquid from running off the pizza.

# NUT CRACKER PIE

This crazy dessert uses a kids' favorite snack—crackers—but tastes just like rich pecan pie!

- **Serves:** 10
- **Time:** 20 minutes to prepare
  30 minutes to bake
- **Complexity:** Easy

## INGREDIENTS

- 14 crackers, such as Ritz
- ⅔ cup walnuts
- 3 egg whites
- ¾ cup sugar
- ¼ teaspoon baking powder
- Low-fat whipping cream or whipped topping
- Vegetable spray

## MATERIALS

- Blender or food chopper
- Mixer
- Deep-dish pie pan

## WHAT TO DO

**1** Preheat oven to 325 degrees.

**2** Crush crackers to a fine powder.

**3** Chop walnuts in the blender or food chopper and mix with crackers.

**4** Beat egg whites until partly stiff.

**5** Slowly add sugar, along with baking powder, to egg whites, and continue to beat.

**6** Fold crackers and nuts into mixture and spread into pie pan sprayed with vegetable spray.

**7** Bake at 325 degrees for 30 minutes. Cool.

**8** Top with whipped cream or whipped topping and refrigerate until serving time.

**VARIATIONS:** You can substitute other nuts for the walnuts, and try different crackers, too.

**PRACTICAL TIPS:** To crush the crackers, place 4 or 5 between two pieces of wax paper and roll with rolling pin. Or place in a small bowl and crush with a fork.

# MONKEY PUDDING

**I**f you want to keep dessert simple but tasty and nutritious, whip up this crowd-pleasing peanut butter and banana pudding. The preparation takes only minutes and the monkeys—and kids—love it!

• **Serves:** 8          • **Time:** 10 minutes to prepare          **Complexity:** Easy

## INGREDIENTS

- 4 bananas, cut into chunks
- 4 cups low-fat vanilla or banana yogurt
- 4 cups low-fat, low-sugar smooth peanut butter

## MATERIALS

- Blender
- 8 dessert cups

## WHAT TO DO

**1** Combine half of each ingredient in blender.

**2** Whirl until smooth.

**3** Repeat steps 1 and 2 with the remaining ingredients.

**4** Pour into individual dessert cups and refrigerate until serving time.

**VARIATIONS:** Replace bananas with applesauce for a unique combination, or use a variety of yogurt flavors.

**PRACTICAL TIPS:** Stir the mixture in the blender several times to make sure it's well blended. Blending half the ingredients at a time prevents overflow.

# ZEBRA DEZZERT

This unusual dessert looks like a zebra! Your guests will have as much fun taking it apart as you had putting it together.

- **Serves:** 6
- **Time:** 20 minutes to prepare
  1 hour to chill
- **Complexity:** Easy

## INGREDIENTS

- 1 package chocolate wafer cookies (about 36)
- 3 cups nondairy or low-fat whipped topping
- 12 chocolate chips

## MATERIALS

- 6 dessert plates

## WHAT TO DO

**1** Spread whipped cream or topping on one cookie.

**2** Top with another cookie and spread it with whipped cream.

**3** Continue until you have a stack of 6 (or more) cookies and cream.

**4** Repeat steps 1, 2, and 3 until you have 6 stacks. Lay each stack of cookies on its side on a dessert plate.

**5** Cover front and back of each stack with remaining whipped cream.

**6** Add two eyes to the front of each zebra using two chocolate chips.

**7** Chill in refrigerator for 1 hour or more.

**VARIATIONS:** Sprinkle tiny chocolate chips all over the zebra's body if you want a spotted zebra. Flavor the whipped cream with a few drops of peppermint extract for a zippy flavor. Tint the whipped topping to make the zebras more colorful.

**PRACTICAL TIP:** Make sure your whipped topping is stiff. Cool Whip-type toppings work best.

# Fun Food Favors

The treats don't have to end just because the party's over. Why not send your guests home with an edible treasure they can share with family and friends. You might hand out small packages of cookies or crackers; give them some fruit rolls or bars; let them take home a bag of popcorn or peanuts; or provide them with a packaged mix, such as brownies or muffins, they can concoct with mom and dad at home.

We've created some fun-to-make and fun-to-take food favors you might want to try, to give your party guests something memorable to take home after the festivities come to an end.

# Fun Food Favors

# ANT FARM

**T**his funny take-home treat looks just like a bagful of sand—with ants! What kid wouldn't love a handful?!

- **Serves:** 8
- **Time:** 15 minutes to prepare
- **Complexity:** Easy

## Ingredients

- 16 rectangular graham crackers
- Chocolate sprinkles

## Materials

- 8 plastic resealable sandwich bags

## What To Do

**1** Crush graham crackers to a fine powder.

**2** Put equal portions of crumbs into 8 sandwich bags.

**3** Add chocolate sprinkles to each bag and mix well.

**4** Tell the kids to eat the Ant Farm, using their fingers or a small spoon.

**Variations:** Use raisins for beetles, red hots for ladybugs, or Gummy bugs for other edible vermin.

**Practical Tips:** To crush graham crackers, place between two pieces of wax paper and roll with a rolling pin. Or place graham crackers on a flat surface and crush with a fork.

# CANDY CROWN

Crown the kids with these colorful headdresses as you say good-bye.

• **Serves:** 1          • **Time:** 10 minutes to prepare each          **Complexity:** Easy

## INGREDIENTS
- 12 cellophane-wrapped candies per guest

## MATERIALS
- Several colors of curly ribbon

## WHAT TO DO

**1** Line up two candies next to one another, with paper ends overlapping.

**2** Cut 12 pieces of ribbon, 6 to 8 inches long, in a variety of colors.

**3** Place ribbon underneath paper ends and tie the ends tightly together.

**4** Repeat until you have a length of candies tied together.

**5** Measure length on a child's head to approximate correct size for crown.

**6** Tie ends together with ribbon.

**7** Pull scissors over ribbon to curl.

**8** Crown the guests as they leave the party.

**VARIATIONS:** Include this as a party activity and have the kids make their own crowns. Or make the candies into necklaces, bracelets, or belts.

**PRACTICAL TIP:** Choose candies that have plenty of wrapping on the ends for easy handling.

# CHOCOLATE APPLES

You've heard of caramel apples—we've made Chocolate Apples on a stick. They're pretty, portable, peanut-covered, and perfect for the party's end!

- **Serves:** 12
- **Time:** 30 minutes to prepare 30 minutes to cool
- **Complexity:** Easy

## INGREDIENTS

- 12 medium apples
- ½ cup low-fat margarine
- 2 squares (2 ounces) unsweetened chocolate
- 2 cups brown sugar
- 1 cup light corn syrup
- 1 14-ounce can sweetened condensed milk
- 1 teaspoon vanilla
- 2 cups chopped peanuts

## MATERIALS

- 12 ice-cream sticks
- Large, heavy saucepan
- Candy thermometer
- Wax paper
- Ribbon

## WHAT TO DO

1 Remove stems from apples and insert ice cream sticks.

2 Melt margarine and chocolate over low heat in saucepan.

3 Add sugar, syrup, and milk; mix well.

4 Cook over medium heat, stirring frequently, until candy thermometer reaches 245 degrees (firm-ball stage).

5 Remove from heat and stir in vanilla.

6 Dip apples into chocolate and cover evenly, allowing excess to drip off.

7 Roll apples in chopped peanuts to cover the whole apple or just ends. Then place on wax paper to cool for 30 minutes.

8 Wrap in wax paper, tie with ribbon, and hand one to each guest.

**VARIATIONS:** Use melted caramels. Roll the covered apples in candy sprinkles, coconut, or other toppings.

**PRACTICAL TIPS:** Use a spoon to help spread the chocolate mixture while dipping, for a smooth, even cover.

# COOKIE COLLECTION

**S**end the guests home with dozens of different cookies—and you have to make only one batch. How? Read on and you'll find out!

- **Serves:** 12
- **Time:** 15 minutes to prepare
  10 minutes to bake
- **Complexity:** Easy

## INGREDIENTS

- 1 favorite cookie recipe to make 3 dozen cookies (see pages 208–209 for our cookie recipes)

## MATERIALS

- Decorative plate
- 12 decorative paper plates or cookie tins
- Cellophane wrap
- Ribbon

## WHAT TO DO

**1** Make your favorite cookie recipe, enough for 3 dozen cookies, and ask each guest to bring 3 dozen of their favorite cookies.

**2** Put cookies you baked on decorative plate on party table.

**3** When guests arrive, have them place cookies on the party table.

**4** At the end of the party, give each guest a decorative paper plate or tin and let them walk around the table, collecting 3 cookies from each plate.

**5** When they finish collecting, wrap each plate in cellophane wrap and tie with a ribbon.

**6** Let the guests take home their 3-dozen Cookie Collection!

**VARIATION:** Do the same with cupcakes, asking each guest to bring 1 dozen decorated cupcakes to share.

**PRACTICAL TIPS:** Cookie tins are sturdier and make nice boxes when they're empty, but they're more expensive than paper plates.

# CRUNCHY POPS

Turn one of kids' favorite treats into a portable popsicle!

- **Serves:** 12
- **Time:** 20 minutes to prepare
- **Complexity:** Easy

## INGREDIENTS

- ¼ cup low-fat margarine
- 1 10-ounce package miniature marshmallows
- 6 cups Rice Krispies cereal
- 1 cup M&Ms (optional)

## MATERIALS

- Large heavy saucepan
- Spoon
- 12 5-ounce decorative drinking cups (wax-lined)
- 12 ice-cream sticks

## WHAT TO DO

1 In large saucepan, melt margarine and marshmallows together, stirring constantly.

2 Pour cereal and M&Ms into melted marshmallow mixture and stir well.

3 Spoon into paper cups and press lightly to fill.

4 Insert sticks in the center and press mixture once more.

5 Cool. Then pass out Crunchy Pops to the departing kids.

**VARIATIONS:** Add ½ cup peanut butter to punch up the flavor a little. Add chocolate chips or raisins to mixture instead of M&Ms.

**PRACTICAL TIP:** Use wax paper cups so the Crunchy Pops will come out easily.

# EDIBLE JEWELRY

Unfortunately, these lovely necklaces and bracelets won't last long. They taste too good to wear!

- **Serves:** 8
- **Time:** 20 minutes to prepare
- **Complexity:** Easy

## INGREDIENTS

- 4 cups of a variety of donut-shaped cereals, such as Trix, Cap'n Crunch, Cinnamon Cheerios, and so on
- 8 thin licorice whips

## MATERIALS

- Small bowls, 1 for each cereal

## WHAT TO DO

**1** Pour cereals into individual bowls and set on table.

**2** Tie one end of each licorice whip into a knot to keep the cereal from falling off, and offer each guest a length of thin licorice.

**3** Have the guests string the cereals onto the licorice any way they like, to make necklace or bracelet.

**4** Tie ends of licorice whip together in a double knot to form necklace.

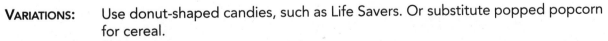

**VARIATIONS:** Use donut-shaped candies, such as Life Savers. Or substitute popped popcorn for cereal.

**PRACTICAL TIP:** Have a bowl of mixed cereal available for the kids to munch on while they string their necklaces.

# MAKE-A-MONSTER DOUGH

Your guests are supposed to play with this creative snack before they eat it!

- **Serves:** 8
- **Time:** 15 minutes to prepare
- **Complexity:** Easy

## INGREDIENTS

- 1 cup low-fat, low-sugar smooth peanut butter
- ½ cup honey
- 1 cup instant nonfat dry milk
- Nuts, seeds, small candies, red hots, raisins, coconut, Cheerios, granola, chocolate chips, and other edible decorations

## MATERIALS

- Spoon
- 8 plastic lunch bags

## WHAT TO DO

**1** Mix peanut butter with honey.

**2** Add dry instant milk until you have a dough-like consistency.

**3** Divide dough into 8 pieces and give 1 piece to each guest.

**4** Let them make monsters out of their dough, using the edible decorations.

**5** Place monsters in plastic bags and send them home with your guests.

**VARIATIONS:** Premake the monsters and give them to your guests as they leave.

**PRACTICAL TIPS:** The dough should not be too dry or too sticky, so add the dry milk accordingly.

# MOUSE CAKES

**M**ickey Mouse would love these Mouse Cakes—and so will your guests! Give them one to eat at the party—and one to take home for a special treat!

- **Serves:** 12
- **Time:** 20 minutes to prepare
  20 minutes to bake
- **Complexity:** Easy

## INGREDIENTS

- 1 package chocolate cake mix
- 1 package white cake mix
- 1 can low-fat cream cheese frosting (or see page 211 for our recipe)
- 24 Oreo cookies
- Red hots
- 12 pieces of thin licorice whips

## MATERIALS

- Cupcake tin
- Cupcake liners
- 12 toothpicks

## WHAT TO DO

**1** Bake 1 dozen chocolate cupcakes, according to package directions. Cool.

**2** Bake 1 dozen white cupcakes, according to package directions. Cool and remove cupcake liners from both chocolate and white cupcakes.

**3** Frost top of chocolate cupcake, and place white cupcake upside-down on top of chocolate cupcake. Secure with a toothpick.

**4** Frost white cupcake with white cream cheese frosting, leaving chocolate cupcake unfrosted.

**5** Stick 2 Oreo cookies into top cupcake to make mouse ears. Then press red hots into frosting on side of top cupcake to make eyes and nose.

**6** Insert short lengths of licorice on either side of nose to make whiskers.

**7** Hand Mouse Cakes to your guests as they head for home.

**VARIATIONS:** Use this as a party treat and substitute vanilla frozen yogurt for white cupcake.

**PRACTICAL TIPS:** If you prefer not to use toothpicks, cut ice-cream sticks in half and use them to anchor the two cupcakes together. Leave the cupcake liner on the chocolate cupcake so your guests have something to hold onto without making a mess.

# SECRET STASH CHIPMUNK CHOW

Send the little critters out the door with our special Chipmunk Chow so they can store it away for the winter—or eat it on the way home!

- **Serves:** 8
- **Time:** 20 minutes to prepare
- **Complexity:** Easy

## INGREDIENTS

- ½ cup popcorn, unpopped
- ⅛ cup low-fat margarine
- ⅛ cup Parmesan cheese
- ½ cup Rice Krispies, Cheerios, or other unsweetened cereal
- ½ cup unsalted peanuts, chopped
- ½ cup walnuts or almonds, chopped
- ½ cup small pretzels
- ½ cup raisins
- ½ cup dried apricots, chopped

## MATERIALS

- Large paper bag
- 8 plastic sandwich bags or other snack holders
- Ribbons

## WHAT TO DO

**1** Pop popcorn and season with low-fat margarine and Parmesan cheese.

**2** Combine popcorn with remaining ingredients in large paper bag and shake well.

**3** Pour into individual bags, seal, and tie at top with ribbon.

**VARIATIONS:** Add your favorite seasonings to the ingredients: Mexican seasoning, pizza seasoning, Deluxe Salad seasoning, powdered cheese packets, or parsley and paprika.

**PRACTICAL TIP:** Offer the kids large sandwich bags or freezer bags so they can grip them more easily.

# TAKE-ALONG TEDDIES

Let the kids make and take these tasty Teddies, or make them yourself and surprise the guests as they go.

- **Serves:** 8
- **Time:** 20 minutes to prepare
  10 minutes to bake
- **Complexity:** Easy

## INGREDIENTS

- 4 packages refrigerator biscuits
- Vegetable spray
- Poppy seeds and/or sesame seeds
- Raisins

## MATERIALS

- Aluminum foil
- Cookie sheet
- Ribbon

## WHAT TO DO

**1** Divide each package of refrigerator biscuits in half.

**2** Knead each half on a sheet of foil to form 8 round lumps of dough.

**3** Divide each of the 8 lumps of dough into 1 large round for body, 1 small round for head, and 8 smaller balls for ears, hands, feet, nose, and tail.

**4** Place bodies on cookie sheet sprayed with vegetable spray.

**5** Place a head above each body.

**6** Add ears at the top of each head, arms at the sides of each body, feet at the bottom of each body, a tail at the lower back, and a nose on the lower half of each head.

**7** Poke raisins into centers of ears, center of noses, above noses to make eyes, and into center of each body to make belly buttons. Add more to hands and feet to make claws, if you like. Sprinkle the rest of the body with poppy or sesame seeds to make "fur."

**8** Bake according to package directions, until golden brown.

**9** Cool, tie ribbon around neck of each Teddie, and give to guests.

**VARIATIONS:** Instead of bears, make puppies, kittens, turtles, pigs, or whatever you like. Let the kids make their own as a party activity.

**PRACTICAL TIPS:** For easy handling, make the bears on foil. Then transfer the foil to cookie sheets.

# Holiday Recipes

# NEW YEAR'S EVE TREATS

The kids can begin the new year with a New Year's Eve party, complete with healthy treats and bubbling drinks! For a champagne-like celebration, offer the kids sparkling apple cider and serve it in stemmed glasses with a cherry at the bottom. Then give them a few fun snacks to wash down.

Here are some New Year's Eve party recipes to help you start the year off with a bang—and a crunch and a chomp and a slurp!

Happy New Year!

# CONFETTI POPCORN BALLS

Instead of tossing confetti on New Year's Eve, make edible confetti and gobble it down at the stroke of midnight!

- **Serves:** 8
- **Time:** 30 minutes to prepare
- **Complexity:** Easy

## INGREDIENTS

- Vegetable spray
- 4 cups popcorn, popped
- 1 cup multicolored gumdrops, chopped
- ½ cup peanuts, chopped
- 3 cups miniature marshmallows
- 3 tablespoons low-fat margarine

## MATERIALS

- Large bowl
- Large heavy saucepan
- Spoon

## WHAT TO DO

**1** Spray large bowl with vegetable spray.

**2** Combine popcorn, gumdrops, and peanuts in bowl.

**3** Combine marshmallows and margarine in large saucepan and melt over medium heat, stirring constantly.

**4** Pour marshmallow mixture over popcorn, candy, and nuts, and toss until coated.

**5** With buttered hands, shape popcorn mixture into 8 balls.

**6** Allow to set until serving time.

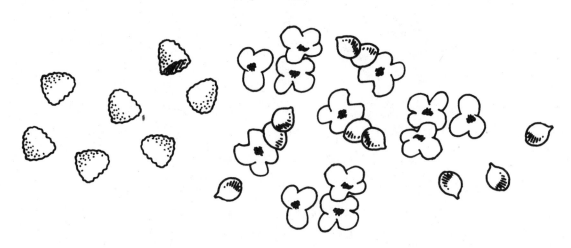

**VARIATIONS:** Use Gummy Bears, M&Ms, small fruit snacks, or other colorful additives instead of gumdrops.

**PRACTICAL TIP:** Work quickly to shape balls before mixture cools and hardens.

# Funny Fortune Cookies

Predict a funny, fantastic future with these Funny Fortune Cookies!

- **Serves:** 8
- **Time:** 30 minutes to prepare
  5 to 10 minutes to cook
- **Complexity:** Moderate

## Ingredients
- ¼ cup flour
- 2 tablespoons sugar
- 1 tablespoon cornstarch
- Dash salt
- 2 tablespoons cooking oil
- 1 egg white
- 1 tablespoon water
- Vegetable spray

## Materials
- 8 strips of colored paper
- Pen
- Medium bowl
- Tablespoon
- Skillet
- Paper towels

## What To Do

1 Write funny fortunes, such as "You will find happiness at a bowling alley," "You will fall in love with a prince who is really a frog," "You will inherit a haunted house" and so on, on each strip of colored paper. Set aside.

2 Combine flour, sugar, cornstarch, and salt in bowl.

3 Add oil and egg white, and stir until smooth. Add water; mix well.

4 Make 1 cookie at a time by pouring 1 tablespoon of batter onto hot skillet sprayed with vegetable spray. Allow it to spread to a 3½-inch circle.

5 Cook over medium heat for 4 minutes, until lightly browned. Turn and cook 1 minute more.

6 Place cookie on paper towel and blot.

7 Place paper fortune in center, and fold cookie in half. Fold again over the edge of a bowl to make fortune cookie shape. Cool.

**Variations:** Color the batter with food coloring for variety. Instead of fortunes, write jokes.

**Practical Tip:** You can make as many cookies at a time as will fit in the skillet. But you must work quickly before the cookies become firm.

# PINK CHAMPAGNE PUNCH

Serve these pretty pink drinks in fancy champagne glasses to toast in the New Year!

- **Serves:** 8
- **Time:** 15 minutes to prepare
- **Complexity:** Easy

### INGREDIENTS

- 1 12-ounce bottle white grape juice
- 1 6-ounce can frozen lemonade concentrate, thawed
- 1 16-ounce package frozen whole strawberries, thawed
- 1 12-ounce can lemon-lime soda, chilled
- 8 cherries (optional)

### MATERIALS

- Blender
- Large drink container
- 8 fancy glasses

### WHAT TO DO

**1** Combine ½ of the grape juice, lemonade, and strawberries in blender.

**2** Whirl until smooth and pour into drink container.

**3** Repeat steps 1 and 2 with remaining juice, lemonade, and strawberries.

**4** Add soda and stir well.

**5** Pour into glasses.

**6** Add a cherry to the glass (optional).

**VARIATION:** You can substitute regular grape juice for white grape juice.

**PRACTICAL TIPS:** Add more soda if you want a less-slushy drink. Use plastic champagne glasses; they look great and won't break.

# SPARKLING FRUIT SUNDAE

This fancy, festive, and fruity dessert is perfect for New Year's Eve.

- **Serves:** 8
- **Time:** 20 minutes to prepare
- **Complexity:** Easy

## INGREDIENTS

- 1 cup red, green, or purple seedless grapes
- 1 10-ounce can mandarin orange slices, drained
- 1 8-ounce can pineapple chunks (drained, but keep the juice)
- 1 pear, apple, or ½ melon, cubed
- 1 banana, sliced
- ¼ cup orange juice
- 1 cup sparkling apple cider

## MATERIALS

- Large bowl
- 8 dessert bowls
- Spoon

## WHAT TO DO

**1** Combine grapes, oranges, pineapple, pear, and banana in bowl.

**2** Put equal portions of fruit into each dessert bowl.

**3** Combine pineapple juice (drained from the can), orange juice, and sparkling apple cider.

**4** Pour juice into each dessert bowl and stir gently.

**VARIATIONS:** Substitute ginger ale or other bubbly drink for apple cider. Use any fruits you like to make your fruit sundae.

**PRACTICAL TIPS:** Refrigerate fruit for half an hour to blend flavors before adding sparkling apple cider.

# WINTER SNOWBALLS

Serve these white winter-time snacks with a glass of hot chocolate or warm apple cider.

- **Serves:** 8 (4 per person)
- **Time:** 20 minutes to prepare 1 hour to cool
- **Complexity:** Easy

## INGREDIENTS

- 1 12-ounce package white chocolate or vanilla chips
- ½ cup walnuts or peanuts, chopped
- ½ cup dates, chopped
- ½ cup cherries, chopped
- 16 cherries, cut in half

## MATERIALS

- Cookie sheet
- Wax paper
- Medium heavy saucepan
- Spoon
- Teaspoon

## WHAT TO DO

**1** Cover cookie sheet with wax paper.

**2** Melt chips in saucepan and stir until smooth.

**3** Stir nuts, dates, and cherries into melted chips.

**4** Drop by teaspoons onto cookie sheet to form snowballs.

**5** Place half cherry in center of each ball.

**6** Refrigerate until serving time.

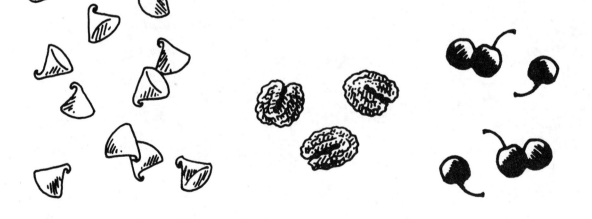

**VARIATIONS:** Tint the white chocolate or vanilla chips different colors for a rainbow effect.

**PRACTICAL TIP:** Refrigerate about 1 hour to set cookies.

# VALENTINE'S DAY SWEETS

Sweets for the sweethearts on Valentine's Day, but you don't have to put cavities into your guests' teeth while putting smiles on their faces. Instead, make your own valentine "candies," using such healthy alternatives as dried fruit, nuts, and cereals, dipped in chocolate, caramel, or vanilla chips. Or give your guests a box filled with fruit treats, raisins, sugar-free gum, or chocolate-dipped pretzels.

To get your ideas flowing, we've provided some of our favorite low-sugar, high-fun recipes. So while the kids are making cards to send to all their friends and loved ones, whip up some good-for-you goodies to keep their energy up.

Happy Valentine's Day!

# BLACK FOREST CAKE

**Q**uick and easy, moist and delicious, with a cherry surprise inside!

- **Serves:** 12
- **Time:** 10 minutes to prepare
  30 minutes to bake
- **Complexity:** Easy

## INGREDIENTS

- 1 12-ounce package frozen cherries, thawed and drained
- 1 package chocolate cake mix
- Vegetable spray
- 1 large container nondairy whipped topping
- Red sprinkles (optional)

## MATERIALS

- Spoon
- Heart-shaped or rectangular cake pan
- 12 dessert plates

## WHAT TO DO

**1** Prepare chocolate cake mix according to package directions.

**2** Stir cherries into cake batter.

**3** Pour mixture into cake pan sprayed with vegetable spray.

**4** Bake according to package directions, cool, and remove from pan.

**5** Top with whipped topping. Add red sprinkles, if desired.

**6** Cut into squares and serve.

**VARIATONS:** Frost cake with low-fat chocolate frosting or cream cheese frosting tinted pink. Using decorator tubes, write "Happy Valentine's Day" or sayings borrowed from candy hearts, such as "Kiss Me," "Say Yes," "Be Mine," "Love Ya," and so on. Or top with red hots, candy hearts, or tiny chocolate chips. Use cherry pie filling in place of frozen cherries, for a richer taste.

**PRACTICAL TIPS:** Completely cool cake before covering with whipped topping. If you bake the cake ahead of time, cover with whipped topping just before serving.

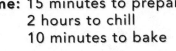

# HEART-TO-HEART COOKIES

Have a heart-to-heart with your loved ones by baking these love-ly heart-shaped cookies!

- **Makes:** 24 cookies
- **Time:** 15 minutes to prepare
  2 hours to chill
  10 minutes to bake
- **Complexity:** Easy

## INGREDIENTS

- ½ cup low-fat margarine
- ½ cup vegetable oil
- ¾ cup low-fat, low-sugar peanut butter
- 1 egg
- 1½ cups sugar
- 1 teaspoon vanilla
- 3 cups flour
- 2 tablespoons low-fat milk
- Food coloring, red
- Flour (for rolling dough)
- Vegetable spray
- Jam, red, any flavor

## MATERIALS

- Large bowl
- Mixer or spoon
- Rolling pin
- Heart-shaped cookie cutter
- Cookie sheet
- Knife

## WHAT TO DO

**1** Combine margarine, oil, and peanut butter in a bowl and mix well.

**2** Add egg to peanut butter mixture and beat well.

**3** Add sugar, vanilla, flour, milk, and red food coloring and mix well.

**4** Chill 2 hours or more, covered.

**5** Preheat oven to 350 degrees.

**6** Roll dough on floured surface to ¼-inch thickness and cut out heart shapes with cookie cutter.

**7** Place on cookie sheet sprayed with vegetable spray and bake at 350 degrees for 8 to 10 minutes.

**8** Cool, spread with jam, and sandwich 2 cookies together.

**VARIATON:** Frost cookies with cream cheese frosting and decorate with frosting tubes.

**PRACTICAL TIP:** Dust cookie cutter with flour every few cuts to keep dough from sticking.

# PINK DRINK

The perfect drink on this cheery, cherry day!

- **Serves:** 8
- **Time:** 10 minutes to prepare
- **Complexity:** Easy

## INGREDIENTS
- 2 cups low-fat vanilla or strawberry yogurt
- 1 cup frozen strawberries
- 2 cups low-fat milk
- 8 cherries

## MATERIALS
- Blender
- 8 fancy glasses

## WHAT TO DO

**1** Combine half the yogurt, strawberries, and milk in blender.

**2** Whirl until smooth.

**3** Pour equal amounts into 4 glasses.

**4** Repeat steps 1, 2, and 3 with remaining yogurt, strawberries, and milk.

**5** Add cherries to each glass and serve.

**VARIATON:** Add a scoop of strawberry low-fat frozen yogurt to turn the Pink Drink into a Fruit Float.

**PRACTICAL TIPS:** If consistency of drink seems too thick to your taste, thin with more milk. Use plastic fancy glasses to prevent breakage.

# SWEETHEART SANDWICHES

The party guests will be surprised and delighted when you bring out these pink Sweetheart Sandwiches for snack time!

- **Serves:** 8
- **Time:** 1 day to order 20 minutes to prepare
- **Complexity:** Easy

## INGREDIENTS

- 1 loaf light whole-wheat or white bread, tinted pink
- ½ cup low-sugar strawberry or raspberry jam
- 3 soft, ripe bananas, mashed, or ½ cup low-fat cream cheese, softened

## MATERIALS

- Heart-shaped cookie cutter
- Knife

## WHAT TO DO

**1** Order tinted bread from bakery a day ahead of time and have it sliced sandwich style; or make your own, using red food coloring.

**2** Use cookie cutter to cut slices into heart shapes.

**3** Spread half of all slices with jam and the rest of all slices with mashed banana or cream cheese.

**4** Combine jam slices with banana or cream cheese slices to make sandwiches.

**Variaton:** Substitute low-fat turkey bologna and low-fat white cheese for jam and bananas.

**Practical Tip:** Cut the leftover scraps into bite-sized pieces and place in a napkin-covered basket. Serve as a snack.

# WIGGLE HEARTS

**W**atch these Wiggle Hearts wobble in the fingers and tickle on the tongue.

- **Serves:** 12
- **Time:** 20 minutes to prepare 2 hours to chill
- **Complexity:** Easy

## INGREDIENTS

- 2 6-ounce packages sugar-free strawberry Jell-O
- 4 envelopes unflavored gelatin

## MATERIALS

- Large rectangular pan
- Heart-shaped cookie cutter
- Wax paper
- Large serving platter or 12 dessert plates

## WHAT TO DO

**1** Make Jell-O according to package directions and add the 4 envelopes of unflavored gelatin.

**2** Pour into large pan and allow to set in the refrigerator 2 hours or more.

**3** When set, cut out heart shapes with cookie cutter and turn out onto wax paper.

**4** Serve on large platter or individual plates and let the kids eat the Wiggle Hearts with their fingers.

**VARIATONS:** Use any flavor of red Jell-O you like.

**PRACTICAL TIPS:** When you're finished cutting out the heart shapes, turn them out onto wax paper all at once. Save scraps to eat.

# ST. PATRICK'S CELEBRATION

After the kids change into their Greens and kiss the Blarney Stone, they can eat the pot of party goodies—just use our fun recipes to create a St. Patrick's Day feast and enjoy the wear'n'—and the eatin'—o' the green! And to make the whole day extraspecial, turn plain old food into fun by simply tinting everything green—from the morning milk to the evening's ice cream.

# EATIN' O' THE GREEN

You've heard of wearin' o' the green? Now it's time for Eatin' o' the Green! Even the kids will eat this Green—just don't tell them what it is!

- **Serves:** 8
- **Time:** 15 minutes to prepare
  2 hours to chill
- **Complexity:** Easy

## INGREDIENTS

- 1 cup low-fat sour cream
- 1 cup low-fat mayonnaise
- ¼ cup green onions, finely chopped
- 1 10-ounce package frozen chopped spinach, thawed and drained
- 1 8-ounce can water chestnuts, drained and finely chopped
- Cut-up vegetables, whole-wheat or sourdough bread cubes, or whole-wheat crackers

## MATERIALS

- Medium bowl
- Serving bowl and platter

## WHAT TO DO

**1** Combine sour cream, mayonnaise, and green onions in bowl. Blend thoroughly.

**2** Stir spinach and water chestnuts into sour cream mixture.

**3** Cover and refrigerate 2 hours or more.

**4** Serve dip in bowl with a platter of veggies, bread, or crackers.

**VARIATION:** Place the dip in individual dessert cups and serve it to your guests with their own plates of dippers.

**PRACTICAL TIP:** The longer you refrigerate the dip, the better the flavors blend.

# LEPRECHAUN BARS

Share these Leprechaun Bars with the lucky guests who come wearing green!

- **Makes:** 3 dozen
- **Time:** 20 minutes to prepare
  35 minutes to bake
  2½ hours to chill
- **Complexity:** Easy

## INGREDIENTS

- 1½ cups low-sugar, low-fat graham cracker cookies, crushed
- 3 tablespoons low-fat margarine, melted
- Vegetable spray
- 1 cup low-fat cream cheese, softened
- 1 14-ounce can sweetened condensed milk
- ¼ cup Key lime juice
- 36 large green gumdrops, sliced into thirds

## MATERIALS

- 9-inch square pan
- Mixer

## WHAT TO DO

1. Mix crushed graham crackers with melted margarine. Press into bottom and up sides of pan sprayed with vegetable spray and refrigerate for 30 minutes.

2. Preheat oven to 350 degrees.

3. Beat cream cheese until light and fluffy.

4. Gradually beat in sweetened condensed milk until smooth. Then beat in lime juice.

5. Spread cream cheese mixture over graham cracker crust.

6. Bake at 350 degrees for 35 minutes, until set.

7. Refrigerate 2 hours or more.

8. Cut into 1-by-1-inch squares and top each square with three gumdrop slices arranged to look like a three-leaf clover.

**VARIATIONS:** Top with sliced kiwi or sliced green grapes.

**PRACTICAL TIP:** Use regular lime juice if you don't have Key lime juice.

# LUCKY CLOVERS

Start St. Patrick's Day off right with these Lucky Clover hotcakes!

- **Serves:** 6
- **Time:** 20 minutes to prepare
- **Complexity:** Easy

## INGREDIENTS

- 2 cups pancake mix and required ingredients
- Food coloring, green
- Vegetable spray
- Low-sugar mint jelly, low-fat lime yogurt, or syrup
- Green candy sprinkles (optional)

## MATERIALS

- Large mixing bowl
- Griddle or skillet
- Tablespoon
- Serving plate
- 6 medium plates

## WHAT TO DO

**1** Mix pancake batter in bowl according to package directions.

**2** Tint batter with green food coloring.

**3** Spray skillet with vegetable spray; heat.

**4** For each hotcake, drop three tablespoons of batter in skillet so they connect in the center to form clover shape.

**5** Cook for 1½ minutes, until lightly browned. Carefully turn and cook another minute or so.

**6** Remove from heat and place on serving plate.

**7** Serve with low-sugar mint jelly, low-fat lime yogurt, or syrup, and sprinkle with green candy sprinkles, if desired.

**VARIATION:** To make Gold Doubloon pancakes, tint the batter yellow, drop by teaspoons into skillet to make miniature rounds, and serve a plate piled high.

**PRACTICAL TIP:** Make three separate small, round pancakes in the griddle and assemble them on the plate to form clover.

# RAINBOW POT OF GOLD

To find the rainbow, your guests won't have to look farther than these nutritious, colorful fruit cups!

- **Serves:** 8
- **Time:** 20 minutes to prepare
- **Complexity:** Easy

## INGREDIENTS

- 2 kiwis, peeled and sliced; or 1 casaba melon, cut into chunks
- 1 cup blueberries
- 1 cup seedless purple grapes
- 1 cup strawberries, sliced
- 1 cup mandarin orange slices
- 2 bananas, sliced
- 1 8-ounce container low-fat vanilla yogurt or 1 cup nondairy whipped topping
- Multicolored candy sprinkles or chocolate gold coins (optional)

## MATERIALS

- 8 parfait glasses or dessert dishes
- Spoon

## WHAT TO DO

**1** Layer kiwi slices or casaba chunks at the bottom of glasses.

**2** Add a layer of blueberries, followed by grapes, strawberry slices, orange slices, and banana slices.

**3** Cover with a spoonful of yogurt or whipped topping.

**4** Garnish with multicolored sprinkles or a chocolate gold coin (1 for each glass).

**VARIATIONS:** After each layer of fruit, spoon in a thin layer of yogurt or whipped topping. Or use frozen yogurt for an ice-cold dessert.

**PRACTICAL TIP:** Use transparent glasses or dessert cups so your guests can see the "rainbow."

# EMERALD CAKE

The surprise hidden at the bottom of this emerald treat makes this dessert a real treasure!

- **Serves:** 8
- **Time:** 20 minutes to prepare
  2 hours to freeze
  3 to 5 minutes to bake
- **Complexity:** Easy

## INGREDIENTS

- 8 individual sponge cakes
- ½ cup mint jelly
- 1 quart mint-chip low-fat frozen yogurt or lime sherbet, softened
- 6 egg whites
- 2 7-ounce jars marshmallow creme
- Food coloring, green
- 8 gold coins (optional)

## MATERIALS

- Cookie sheet
- Ice-cream scoop or spoon
- Mixer
- 8 dessert plates

## WHAT TO DO

**1** Place sponge cakes on cookie sheet and spread with mint jelly.

**2** Place 1 scoop of frozen yogurt or sherbet in the center of each cake. Freeze until firm.

**3** Beat egg whites to soft peaks.

**4** Gradually add marshmallow creme and green food coloring to egg whites, beating until stiff peaks form.

**5** Remove cakes from freezer and spread meringue over frozen yogurt and cake, covering completely. Freeze until serving time.

**6** To serve, remove from freezer, and bake at 500 degrees for 3 to 5 minutes, until lightly browned.

**7** Place gold coins on dessert plates and place cakes on top. Tell your guests there's a surprise at the bottom.

**VARIATION:** Add green sprinkles to the top of the meringue for an added sparkle.

**PRACTICAL TIP:** You can make the meringues without the marshmallow creme, but the creme helps meringue hold its shape.

# EASTER EDIBLES

For a lot of families, Easter time is eating time. For the kids, that often means marshmallow eggs, sugar bunnies, and chocolate chicks. While the sweet stuff is fine in moderation, why not create some Easter treats that are more nutritious, still delicious, and cute as a bunny in a basket! Here are some egg-ceptional recipes to try during the Easter holidays, so hop to it!

# Bunny In A Basket

Create this adorable Bunny in a Basket treat and your guests won't even know they've just eaten a nutritious salad!

- **Serves:** 6
- **Time:** 20 minutes to prepare
- **Complexity:** Easy

## Ingredients

- 3 cups lettuce, shredded
- 6 canned pear halves
- 6 canned peach halves
- 6 bananas, sliced in half lengthwise
- 24 canned prune halves
- 12 raisins
- 6 cherries
- 1 carrot, sliced into thin strips the size of a toothpick

## Materials

- 6 dessert plates

## What To Do

**1** Sprinkle ½ cup shredded lettuce over dessert plate to make the basket.

**2** To make front view of bunny, place 1 pear half vertically in center of plate for bunny's body.

**3** Place 1 peach half on top of narrow end of pear for bunny's head.

**4** Place 2 banana halves at the top of the head for bunny ears.

**5** Place 2 prune halves at bottom of body for feet and 2 prune halves at sides for paws.

**6** Add raisins for eyes and a cherry for the nose on bunny's head.

**7** Place carrot strips on head for whiskers.

**8** Repeat steps 1 through 7 to make the rest of Bunny in a Basket salads.

**Variations:** Add shredded carrot to the shredded lettuce to make basket even more nutritious. Sprinkle coconut all over bunny's body to make fur. To make side view of bunny, place peach half (head) next to pear half (body), place 2 prune halves at bottom for feet, and place a marshmallow at back for tail.

**Practical Tip:** Let your guests make their own bunnies, following your directions.

# CHEWY GOOEY EGGS

These may look like Easter eggs, but they're full of nutrition! And you can be creative with the ingredients.

- **Serves:** 10
- **Time:** 20 minutes to prepare 10 to 15 minutes to bake
- **Complexity:** Easy

## INGREDIENTS

- 1 10-ounce can flaky dinner biscuits
- ⅛ cup low-sugar apple jelly
- 2 apples, chopped
- ¼ cup raisins
- ¼ cup walnuts, chopped
- 2 tablespoons low-fat margarine
- 1 tablespoon cinnamon
- Food color, any colors

## MATERIALS

- Mixing bowl
- Cookie sheet
- Toothpick, Q-tip, or fine-tip paintbrush

## WHAT TO DO

**1** Preheat oven to 375 degrees.

**2** Separate dinner biscuits and split each one into two halves.

**3** Mix apples, raisins, and nuts; divide into 10 equal portions and place in center of one half of each roll. Add a small amount of margarine and a sprinkle of cinnamon.

**4** Top with other half of roll and seal edges by pinching closed with fingers.

**5** Gently form the roll into egg shape with cupped hands and place on ungreased cookie sheet.

**6** Dip toothpick, Q-tip, or paintbrush into food color and dot dough with colors to form speckles.

**7** Bake at 375 degrees 10 to 15 minutes, until golden brown. Remove from oven; serve.

**VARIATIONS:** You can make these "eggs" into mini-lunch bites by substituting chopped meat and cheese for the fruit and nuts.

**PRACTICAL TIPS:** Allow the rolls to cool a few minutes before serving, since they're hot inside. Keep in mind that the number of rolls may vary from 8 to 12 per package. Make sure you have enough.

# EASTER EGG CAKE

Set this whimsical cake on the Easter table and watch it disappear!

- **Serves:** 10
- **Time:** 20 minutes to prepare
  30 minutes to bake
- **Complexity:** Easy

## INGREDIENTS

- 1 package carrot cake mix or favorite recipe
- Vegetable spray
- 3 cups flaky coconut
- Food color: green, red, blue, and yellow
- 2 cans low-fat cream cheese frosting (or see page 211 for our recipe)

## MATERIALS

- Cupcake tin
- Angel food or bundt cake pan
- Large platter
- 4 plastic bags
- Knife or spatula

## WHAT TO DO

**1** Prepare cake mix according to package directions.

**2** Spray 3 cupcake cups with vegetable spray and fill half full with batter.

**3** Pour remaining batter into angel food or bundt cake pan sprayed with vegetable spray.

**4** Bake both cake and cupcakes until done. Cool, then turn out cake onto large platter.

**5** Place 2 cups of coconut in a plastic bag, add several drops of green food coloring, and shake bag until the coconut is tinted green.

**6** Place ⅓ cup of remaining coconut in plastic bag, add a few drops of red food coloring, and shake bag until coconut turns pink.

**7** Repeat step 6 for remaining coconut, tinting ⅓ blue and ⅓ yellow.

**8** Frost 3 cupcakes with cream cheese frosting.

**9** Cover one cupcake with pink coconut, one with yellow, and one with blue.

**10** Frost cake with remaining cream cheese frosting. Sprinkle green coconut all over cake to make grassy basket.

**11** Insert cupcakes in center of cake to make eggs nestled in basket.

**VARIATION:** Instead of filling center of cake with cupcakes, fill with Easter eggs.

**PRACTICAL TIP:** Spread tinted coconut on paper towel to soak up extra moisture from food coloring.

# POPCORN PETER RABBIT

Make a take-apart Popcorn Peter Rabbit to please your Easter crowd!

- **Serves:** 8
- **Time:** 20 minutes to prepare
- **Complexity:** Easy

## INGREDIENTS

- 6 cups popcorn, popped
- ½ cup tiny Easter candies, such as pastel M&Ms, jelly beans, or Easter eggs
- ⅓ cup coconut
- Vegetable spray
- 2 cups miniature marshmallows
- 3 tablespoons low-fat margarine
- 2 raisins or dates

## MATERIALS

- Large bowl
- Large, heavy saucepan
- Spoon
- Cake pan in the shape of a rabbit (optional)
- Wax paper
- Tubes of frosting (optional)

## WHAT TO DO

**1** Combine popcorn with candies and coconut in large bowl sprayed with vegetable spray.

**2** Combine marshmallows and margarine in saucepan and melt over low heat, stirring constantly.

**3** Pour melted marshmallow mixture over popcorn mixture and toss until evenly coated.

**4** Pour popcorn mixture into rabbit-shaped pan sprayed with vegetable spray, or pour onto counter covered with wax paper and shape into rabbit, making one large ball for head, two long rectangular pieces for ears, and a small ball on top of face for nose.

**5** Decorate face with raisins or, when cool, with tubes of frosting.

**VARIATION:** If a rabbit is too difficult, shape popcorn into a giant Easter egg!

**PRACTICAL TIP:** If you are shaping the rabit with your hands, butter your hands and work quickly before the mixture cools.

# WIGGLE EGGS

Your guests will never figure out how you made these wobbly, colorful eggs!

- **Serves:** 12
- **Time:** 20 minutes to prepare
  3 hours to set
- **Complexity:** Easy

## INGREDIENTS

- Vegetable spray
- 1 3-ounce package of favorite flavor sugar-free Jell-O
- 1 envelope unflavored gelatin

## MATERIALS

- 1 dozen eggs
- Skewer
- Egg carton
- Saucepan
- Bowl
- Funnel

## WHAT TO DO

**1** Use a skewer to poke a hole at the broad end of each egg and to scramble inside of eggs. Shake egg over bowl to make inside drip out.

**2** Rinse each egg place in egg carton to dry.

**3** When eggs are dry, spray inside lightly with vegetable spray.

**4** Prepare Jell-O in saucepan according to package directions, adding extra envelope of unflavored gelatin.

**5** Heat Jell-O over low heat until it is dissolved, remove from heat, and cool to lukewarm.

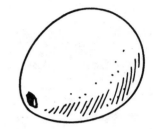

**6** Hold one egg over bowl, hole up; insert funnel and carefully pour Jell-O into egg, filling to the top.

**7** Put egg back in carton, hole up, and repeat step 6 for remaining eggs.

**8** Put Jell-O-filled eggs in refrigerator for 3 hours to set.

**9** At serving time, crack open the eggs and surprise your guests with a handful of wiggley eggs.

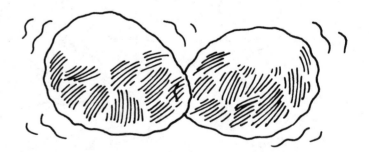

**VARIATIONS:** Give the guests an egg to crack open and peel themselves. Use a variety of Jell-O flavors and colors for a multicolored egg collection.

**PRACTICAL TIPS:** To prevent eggshells from breaking, cool Jell-O to lukewarm before pouring into eggshells.

# PURIM AND PASSOVER PARTIES

Purim, the Festival of Lots, is celebrated in February and March, and commemorates the time when the Jews persuaded the king to change his ruling that would have them all killed. On this special holiday, kids dress up in costumes and exchange edible gifts, such as Poppy Seed Cookies and Carrot-Ginger Candy.

Passover is an eight-day holiday that celebrates the delivery of the Jews from slavery in Egypt more than 3,000 years ago. The holiday takes place in March and/or April (the date varies) and begins with the Seder—a large family dinner during which the family members retell the story of the exodus from Egypt and explain the meaning of the various symbols in the Passover meal. Those observing Passover eat only unleavened bread (matzo) and other specially prepared foods.

Here are a few recipes to try at both holidays to share with family and friends.

# CARROT-GINGER CANDY

These brittle-like candies can be made at Purim, Passover, and Hanukkah.

- **Makes:** 100 small pieces
- **Time:** 30 minutes to prepare
  20 to 30 minutes to cook
  1 hour to set
- **Complexity:** Easy

## INGREDIENTS

- 2 lemons
- 2 cups sugar
- ½ cup water
- ½ teaspoon ginger, ground
- 8 carrots, grated
- 1 cup walnuts, finely chopped

## MATERIALS

- Grater
- Bowl
- Saucepan
- Candy thermometer
- Marble slab
- Spoon

## WHAT TO DO

1. Grate rind of one lemon. Squeeze juice from both lemons into bowl.

2. Combine sugar, water, ginger, lemon rind, and lemon juice in saucepan.

3. Add carrots and bring to a boil over medium heat.

4. Cook 20 to 30 minutes, until liquid is gone and thermometer reaches 240 degrees (hard-ball stage).

5. Remove from heat, stir in chopped nuts, and mix well.

6. Sprinkle a few drops of cold water on marble slab.

7. Pour candy over marble surface and flatten with dampened spoon to form a rough 12-inch square, ⅛-inch thick.

8. While mixture is warm, cut into ¾-inch squares and let stand 1 hour, until firm.

**VARIATION:** Use a wooden board or large flat platter instead of marble slab.

**PRACTICAL TIP:** Wrap leftovers in plastic wrap and store in airtight container.

# HAROSET ON MATZO CRACKERS

Haroset is a popular treat during Passover, full of fruit and nuts.

- **Serves:** 12
- **Time:** 20 minutes to prepare
  30 minutes to chill
- **Complexity:** Easy

## INGREDIENTS

- 1 pound dates, pitted and chopped
- 1½ cups water
- ¼ cup orange juice
- 1 cup walnuts, chopped
- ¼ teaspoon cinnamon
- Matzo crackers

## MATERIALS

- Medium saucepan
- Strainer
- Spoon
- Decorative bowl

## WHAT TO DO

1 Place dates and water in saucepan, cover, and bring to a boil.

2 Reduce heat and simmer 10 minutes, stirring occasionally.

3 Remove from heat and strain dates. Discard water.

4 Place dates back in saucepan, add a little orange juice, and stir until smooth.

5 Stir in remaining orange juice, nuts, and cinnamon.

6 Pour into bowl and chill for 30 minutes or more.

7 Spread on matzo crackers to serve.

**VARIATIONS:** Instead of puréeing the dates, chop them up well but leave mixture chunky.

**PRACTICAL TIP:** The smooth, jam-like consistency is easier to spread and eat.

# NUTTY TORTE

The Nutty Torte makes a great dessert at Passover.

- **Serves:** 12
- **Time:** 20 minutes to prepare
  35 to 45 minutes to bake
- **Complexity:** Easy

## INGREDIENTS

- 4 eggs, separated
- ½ teaspoon salt
- ½ cup sugar
- ¼ cup honey
- ¼ cup orange juice
- ¼ teaspoon cinnamon
- ¾ cup matzo meal
- ¾ cups walnuts, finely ground
- Vegetable spray
- 1 tablespoon powdered sugar
- Low-fat frozen vanilla yogurt

## MATERIALS

- 1 large bowl
- 1 medium bowl
- Mixer
- Spoon
- 8-inch square baking pan
- Wax paper
- Serving plate

## WHAT TO DO

**1** Preheat oven to 350 degrees.

**2** Place 4 egg yolks in large bowl and 4 egg whites in medium bowl.

**3** Beat whites until foamy. Add salt and beat until stiff peaks form.

**4** Beat yolks. Add sugar, honey, juice, and cinnamon. Beat well. Then stir in matzo meal and nuts.

**5** Gently fold nut mixture into egg whites, a spoonful at a time.

**6** Spoon batter into pan sprayed well with vegetable spray and lined with wax paper.

**7** Bake at 350 degrees for 35 to 45 minutes, until done inside.

**8** Cool, turn out onto plate, and remove wax paper.

**9** Dust top with powdered sugar or serve with a scoop of frozen yogurt.

**VARIATION:** To make a fancy design with the powdered sugar, lay a paper doily or other stencil over the cake. Sift sugar over stencil and remove.

**PRACTICAL TIP:** Lining the cake pan with wax paper makes removing the cake easier.

# POPPY-SEED COOKIES

Your guests can help you make this traditional Purim cookie.

- **Makes:** 4 dozen
- **Time:** 10 minutes to prepare
  10 to 12 minutes to bake
- **Complexity:** Easy

## INGREDIENTS

- 2 eggs, separated
- 1 cup sugar
- 1 teaspoon vanilla
- Pinch of salt
- 2 tablespoons poppy seeds
- 1 cup low-fat margarine, melted
- 3 cups flour

## MATERIALS

- Large mixing bowl
- Mixer
- Cookie sheet

## WHAT TO DO

**1** Preheat oven to 350 degrees.

**2** Beat egg yolks in large bowl.

**3** Beat in sugar, vanilla, and salt.

**4** Add poppy seeds and melted margarine. Beat well.

**5** Add flour, 1 cup at a time, beating well after each addition.

**6** Roll dough into balls the size of walnuts, set on ungreased cookie sheet, and press with fork to flatten.

**7** Bake at 350 degrees for 10 to 12 minutes, until lightly browned.

**VARIATION:** Press a raisin into the center of each cookie.

**PRACTICAL TIP:** Allow melted margarine to cool a little before using.

# TRI-CORNER HAT COOKIES

Hamantashen, also called Tri-Corner Hat Cookies, are traditional Purim pastries filled with prunes and shaped into triangles to look like the hat of Haman, the king's evil advisor.

- **Makes:** 2 dozen
- **Time:** 30 minutes to prepare
  12 minutes to bake
- **Complexity:** Easy

## INGREDIENTS

- 2 eggs
- ½ cup sugar
- ½ cup low-fat margarine, melted
- 2 tablespoons water
- 1 teaspoon vanilla
- ½ teaspoon baking soda
- ½ teaspoon baking powder
- Pinch of salt
- 3 cups flour
- 1½ cups cooked pitted prunes, pureed in blender
- 1 tablespoon lemon juice
- ½ cup walnuts, chopped
- ½ cup corn flakes, crushed
- Vegetable spray

## MATERIALS

- Large mixing bowl
- Mixer
- Wax paper
- Rolling pin
- Tablespoon
- Cup or glass (for cutting the dough)
- Cookie sheet

## WHAT TO DO

**1** Beat eggs in mixing bowl; add sugar, margarine, water, and vanilla; and mix well.

**2** Add soda, baking powder, salt, and flour. Stir until ball of dough forms.

**3** Wrap dough in wax paper and chill while making filling.

**4** Preheat oven to 375 degrees.

**5** Mix together prunes, lemon juice, nuts, and cereal.

**6** Remove dough from refrigirator and roll it out on a flat, floured surface or wax paper, to ⅛-inch thickness. Then cut circles out of dough with a cup or glass until dough is used up.

**7** Place tablespoon of filling in center. Flip up 3 sides to make triangle.

**8** Put cookies on sprayed cookie sheet and bake at 375 degrees for 12 minutes.

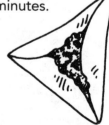

**VARIATIONS:** Add a few drops of honey to top of cookies before baking. Use other fillings, such as apricot, strawberry, and poppy seed.

**PRACTICAL TIP:** Pinch cookies closed to seal them before baking.

# FOURTH OF JULY FAVORITES

The Fourth of July is family time—and food time! It's when all your relatives and friends gather together to celebrate the birthday of America—at the pool, on a picnic, or over the backyard grill. Keep your culinary color scheme red, white, and blue and you'll have a festive time creating patriotic snacks and treats. If you need a few new ideas to help you celebrate the summer holiday, try some of our fun picnic party foods!

# FIRECRACKER SUNDAE

Serve this glow-in-the-dark sundae at night for great special effects! But only under adult supervision!

- **Serves:** 6
- **Time:** 10 minutes to prepare
- **Complexity:** Easy

## INGREDIENTS

- 3 8-ounce containers low-fat vanilla yogurt
- 1 cup strawberries, sliced
- 1 cup blueberries
- 6 tablespoons nondairy whipped topping
- 6 sugar cubes
- Lemon extract

## MATERIALS

- Ice-cream scoop or spoon
- 6 dessert dishes
- Matches

## WHAT TO DO

**1** Scoop ½ container of yogurt into each dessert dish.

**2** Cover with strawberries and blueberries.

**3** Add a spoonful of whipped topping.

**4** Set sugar cube in center of whipped topping.

**5** Pour a little lemon extract on top.

**6** Carefully light a match and light the sugar cube.

**7** Watch flame burn. When flame is extinguished, remove sugar cube and eat the sundae.

**VARIATION:** Use raspberries instead of strawberries.

**PRACTICAL TIP:** Teach the kids the dangers of fire and use caution when lighting matches.

# FRUIT SPARKLERS

Instead of high-fat, high-salt chips and dips, serve these stunning Fruit Sparklers, perfect for the Fourth!

- **Serves:** 8
- **Time:** 20 minutes to prepare
- **Complexity:** Easy

## INGREDIENTS

- 24 large blueberries
- 24 strawberries
- 3 bananas, cut into 8 pieces each
- 24 cherries
- 24 large marshmallows

## MATERIALS

- 8 wooden skewers
- 8 each of red, white, and blue ribbons in 1-foot lengths

## WHAT TO DO

**1** Skewer fruit and marshmallows on wooden skewers in a red, white, and blue pattern, using four of each item on each skewer.

**2** Tie red, white, and blue ribbons to the bottom of the skewer.

**VARIATION:** Cut grapefruit or melon in half and place face down on plate. Stick pointed ends of fruit-filled skewers into grapefruit or melons to make a fancy centerpiece. Let kids remove fruit skewers to eat.

**PRACTICAL TIP:** When finished skewering fruit, break off sharp tips of skewers to prevent injury.

# PATRIOTIC PUNCH

You can be creative with the ice cubes in this fancy punch by using your imagination and your favorite fruits!

- **Serves:** 12
- **Time:** 10 minutes to prepare
  2 hours to freeze
- **Complexity:** Easy

## INGREDIENTS

- 12 cherries or small strawberries
- 12 blueberries
- 2 12-ounce cans frozen lemonade, reconstituted, thawed
- 1 32-ounce bottle sugar-free lemon-lime soda

## MATERIALS

- Ice cube tray
- Large punch bowl
- Ladle
- 12 tall clear glasses

## WHAT TO DO

**1** Put a cherry or strawberry and a blueberry into each ice cube compartment.

**2** Pour 1 can lemonade into the ice cube tray over the fruit. Freeze until firm.

**3** Combine second can of lemonade with soda in punch bowl.

**4** Place lemonade ice cubes in punch bowl.

**5** Serve a lemonade ice cube with each drink in glasses.

**VARIATION:** Instead of putting fruit into ice cubes, tint ice cubes red and blue using food coloring.

**PRACTICAL TIP:** If strawberries are large, slice them.

# PICNIC POPS

**T**hese pops are easy to make, but they do take a little planning and time, so be sure to whip them up the day before your picnic!

- **Serves:** 8
- **Time:** 20 minutes to prepare
  4 hours to freeze
- **Complexity:** Easy

## INGREDIENTS

- 2 cups apple juice
- 4 cups strawberries, fresh or frozen
- 4 cups blueberries, fresh or frozen

## MATERIALS

- Blender
- 2 Popsicle molds
- 12 paper cups
- 12 Popsicle sticks

## WHAT TO DO

**1** Whirl together 1 cup apple juice with strawberries in blender.

**2** Pour liquid into molds or cups, filling half full. Insert sticks and freeze for 2 hours.

**3** Whirl together remaining apple juice with blueberries in blender.

**4** Add liquid to molds or cups that contain the strawberry mixture, filling to the top. Freeze for 2 more hours.

**5** When firm, remove from freezer, remove from molds or peel off cups, and serve.

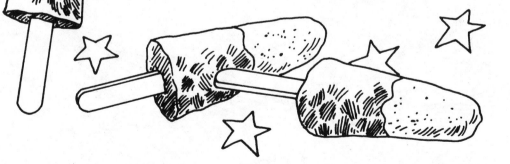

**VARIATIONS:** Alternate the red and blue layers 4 times instead of 2 times. Add a white layer using lemonade or coconut juice.

**PRACTICAL TIP:** To keep the sticks upright before the liquid freezes, cover each paper cup with foil and insert stick through the hole cut in the top.

# RED, WHITE, AND BLUEBERRY CAKE

Make this impressive patriotic cake to please the hungry picnic crowd.

- **Serves:** 12
- **Time:** 10 minutes to prepare
  30 minutes to bake
  20 minutes to decorate
- **Complexity:** Easy

## INGREDIENTS

- 1 package white cake mix
- Vegetable spray
- Food coloring, red and blue
- 1 large container nondairy whipped topping or low-fat whipped cream
- 2 cups strawberries, sliced
- 1 cup blueberries

## MATERIALS

- Large bowl
- 9-by-12-inch cake pan
- Toothpick
- 12 dessert plates

## WHAT TO DO

**1** Prepare cake mix according to package directions and pour into pan sprayed with vegetable spray.

**2** Squeeze a few drops of red and blue food coloring into cake mix and swirl with a toothpick.

**3** Bake cake until done; cool completely.

**4** Cover cake with whipped topping.

**5** Top with strawberries and blueberries in any design you like.

**6** Cut and serve the cake, revealing the red and blue design in each piece!

**VARIATION:** Decorate the cake to look like a flag, by lining up the blueberries in the upper left-hand corner to make stars and creating 1-inch stripes with the strawberry slices.

**PRACTICAL TIP:** Don't frost the cake with the whipped cream until you are ready to serve it, so the whipped cream doesn't melt.

# HALLOWEEN HUNGRIES

Along with Halloween come a porchful of hungry hobgoblins, eager to fill their sacks and tummies with all sorts of snacks and treats. If you're hosting a Halloween party as an alternative to trick or treating, you can serve the kids' favorite snacks—but give them a scary name to make them more fun to eat! Or read on to find some creepy treats that are sure to scare up an appetite.

Happy Halloween!

# "CARAMEL" APPLES

They taste just like regular caramel apples, but they offer better nutrition for the little goblins!

- **Serves:** 8
- **Time:** 20 minutes to prepare
- **Complexity:** Easy

## INGREDIENTS

- 4 Granny Smith apples, sliced and cored
- 1 cup peanut butter
- 1 cup Golden Grahams cereal, crushed

## MATERIALS

- 8 small plastic knives
- 8 small bowls
- 8 small plates

## WHAT TO DO

**1** Give each kid a plastic knife and divide the apple slices among 8 plates.

**2** Have the kids spread peanut butter on one side of the apple slices.

**3** Divide the cereal among 8 bowls.

**4** Have the kids dip the peanut butter side of the apple slices in the crushed cereal and eat.

**VARIATIONS:** Try different crushed cereals for variety.

**PRACTICAL TIPS:** If your guests are young, spread the peanut butter on the apple slices for them, dip the apples in the cereal, and place on plates.

# EYEBALL CAKE

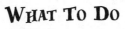

Is this cake really watching you? Or is it just your imagination?

- **Serves:** 12
- **Time:** 20 minutes to prepare
  2 hours to set
- **Complexity:** Easy

## INGREDIENTS

- 1 package chocolate cake mix or favorite chocolate cake recipe
- Vegetable spray
- 1 quart low-fat frozen vanilla yogurt, softened
- 1 quart orange sherbet, softened
- 1 large container nondairy whipped topping
- 1 package chocolate wafer cookies, crushed
- 2 large marshmallows
- 2 raisins
- 12 miniature marshmallows

## MATERIALS

- 9-by-12-inch cake pan
- Knife or spatula (for spreading)

## WHAT TO DO

**1** Prepare cake mix according to package directions, pour into rectangular pan sprayed with vegetable spray, and bake.

**2** When cake is done, remove from pan and cool.

**3** Spread with softened frozen vanilla yogurt and place in freezer to firm.

**4** When the vanilla layer is firm, spread a layer of softened orange sherbet on top and return to freezer.

**5** When the sherbet layer is firm, spread with a layer of whipped topping and top with crushed chocolate wafer cookies.

**6** Make a small hole in each of the large marshmallows and insert raisins in holes to make "pupils" in "eyeballs."

**7** Place eyeballs on cake, near one end.

**8** Place miniature marshmallows underneath in 2 rows of 6 to form toothy grin.

**9** Refreeze until firm and cut into squares.

**VARIATION:**  Use cookie crumbs instead of cake as a crust.

**PRACTICAL TIPS:** Work quickly to keep dessert from melting. Layer the frozen yogurt and sherbet on top of the cake while it's still in the pan, and remove when frozen.

# JACK-O'-LANTERN CUSTARD

Bake your favorite pumpkin pie in these miniature "pumpkin" shells and let your guests have their own Jack-O'-Lantern Custards.

- **Serves:** 6
- **Time:** 20 minutes to prepare
  25 to 35 minutes to bake
- **Complexity:** Easy

## INGREDIENTS

- 6 oranges
- 3 cups canned pumpkin pie mix or your favorite recipe
- 1 stalk of celery

## MATERIALS

- Knife
- Permanent black felt-tip pen
- Large bowl
- Cupcake tin

## WHAT TO DO

**1** Preheat oven to 350 degrees.

**2** Cut tops off oranges in a zigzag pattern. Remove pulp and juice.

**3** Decorate orange shells with jack-o'-lantern faces using permanent felt-tip pen.

**4** Prepare your favorite pumpkin pie recipe in large bowl.

**5** Pour mixture into orange shells and set shells in cupcake tin to balance them.

**6** Bake according to recipe directions for individual servings, about 350 degrees for 25 to 35 minutes, until inserted toothpick comes out clean. Cool.

**7** Cut celery stalk into 6 small stems and insert them into the tops of the Jack-O'-Lantern Custards.

**VARIATION:** Prepare your favorite corn bread recipe and fill orange shells with batter. Bake according to recipe directions and serve Jack-O'-Lantern Corn Bread.

**PRACTICAL TIP:** Thinly slice bottoms of oranges with a knife to make a flat surface for the pumpkin to stand. Don't slice too much or you may poke a hole in the shell.

# PUMPKIN SHAKE

Here's a smooth and creamy shake that matches the orange decorations—and the party mood!
Serve it in individual hollow orange shells with a jack-o'-lantern face drawn on the outside!

- **Serves:** 8
- **Time:** 10 minutes to prepare
- **Complexity:** Easy

## INGREDIENTS

- 8 oranges
- 1 cup canned pumpkin
- 1 cup brown sugar
- 1 teaspoon cinnamon
- ½ teaspoon ground ginger
- ½ teaspoons ground nutmeg
- ½ cup orange juice
- 4 cups low-fat frozen vanilla yogurt

## MATERIALS

- Knife
- Permanent black felt-tip pen
- Blender
- 8 straws

## WHAT TO DO

**1** Cut off tops of oranges, remove pulp (reserving liquid in a measuring cup), and wash and dry the shell.

**2** Draw triangle eyes, nose, and mouth on the orange shells, using a permanent black felt-tip pen.

**3** Combine ingredients (using the reserved orange juice for the ½ cup required) in the blender and whirl until smooth.

**4** Pour shake into oranges and serve with straws.

**VARIATIONS:** Pour shake into a carved-out pumpkin shell, decorated in the same way as the oranges. Use a ladle to serve from the shell. Use glasses instead of orange shells.

**PRACTICAL TIP:** Blend half the ingredients at a time to prevent overflow.

# WORMY APPLES

While these Wormy Apples might disgust most adults, the kids just gobble them up!

- **Serves:** 8
- **Time:** 20 minutes to prepare
  30 minutes to bake
- **Complexity:** Easy

## INGREDIENTS
- 8 red apples
- 1 cup low-fat, low-sugar peanut butter
- 1 cup favorite low-sugar jam
- 8 Gummy Worms

## MATERIALS
- Apple corer (optional)
- Medium bowl
- Spoon
- Cupcake tin
- Large, rectangular pan
- 8 plates

## WHAT TO DO

**1** Preheat oven to 350 degrees.

**2** Remove the apple cores, being careful to leave the bottom of each apple intact.

**3** Combine peanut butter and jelly in bowl.

**4** Stuff mixture into center of apples.

**5** Place apples in cupcake tin, set tin in pan half full of water, and bake at 350 degrees for 30 minutes, until apples are tender.

**6** Cool; then place on individual serving plates.

**7** Insert Gummy Worm halfway into hole, with the rest hanging over the side, and serve.

**VARIATION:** Spoon melted peanut butter and jelly mixture over the apples as a sauce.

**PRACTICAL TIP:** Add Gummy Worms to anything you serve during your Halloween party for that extra icky touch!

# THANKSGIVING GOODIES

Food is the theme for many Americans on Thanksgiving, and family parties offer traditional favorites year after year. This year why not start a new tradition, using healthier foods for better nutrition. You can adapt your treasured family recipes and make them lower in fat and higher in fiber, or you can borrow recipes from other families and expand your heritage on this food-sharing day. Parents and kids can help make some of these Thanksgiving goodies too, which can also become part of the tradition and celebration.

# Corny Pudding

Try this Native American dish that presents corn in a new way.

- **Serves:** 8
- **Time:** 15 minutes to prepare
  30 to 35 minutes to bake
- **Complexity:** Moderate

## Ingredients

- 2 eggs
- ¼ cup low-fat margarine
- ½ cup flour
- 1 cup low-fat milk
- 1 teaspoon salt
- 2 cups corn, fresh, frozen, or canned
- Vegetable spray

## Materials

- 2 medium bowls
- Mixer
- Saucepan
- Spoon (for stirring)
- Baking dish

## What To Do

**1** Preheat oven to 350 degrees.

**2** Separate eggs, beat yolks lightly in 1 bowl, and beat whites in a second bowl until stiff.

**3** Melt margarine in saucepan.

**4** Add flour to margarine and stir over medium heat until thick and smooth.

**5** Add milk to mixture in saucepan and bring to a boil, stirring constantly.

**6** Turn heat to low. Add egg yolks, salt, and corn. Mix well.

**7** Remove saucepan from heat and fold egg whites into corn mixture.

**8** Pour mixture into baking pan sprayed with vegetable spray.

**9** Bake at 350 degrees for 30 to 35 minutes, until lightly browned.

**VARIATIONS:** Add some diced pimento for color. Bake in individual baking dishes for each guest.

**PRACTICAL TIP:** Clean and dry mixer after each use for best results.

# CRANAPPLE CIDER

Heat up this snappy cider to greet your guests and watch the crowd warm up fast!

- **Serves:** 12
- **Time:** 20 minutes to prepare
- **Complexity:** Easy

## INGREDIENTS
- 12 cinnamon sticks
- 1 32-ounce bottle natural apple juice
- 1 32-ounce bottle cranberry juice

## MATERIALS
- Large saucepan
- Coffee mugs
- Cinnamon sticks

## WHAT TO DO

**1** Combine all ingredients in saucepan and bring to a boil.

**2** Simmer 20 minutes or more.

**3** Serve in coffee mugs with cinnamon stick stirrers.

**VARIATION:** Add apricot nectar to make the punch thicker and creamier.

**PRACTICAL TIP:** The longer you simmer the cider, the better the flavors blend.

# CRANBERRY CLOUD

Here's a fancy way to serve up the cranberries—and your guests won't even know they're eating a good-for-you salad!

- **Serves:** 6
- **Time:** 20 minutes to prepare 2 hours to chill
- **Complexity:** Easy

## INGREDIENTS

- 1 envelope unflavored gelatin
- 2 cups hot water
- 1 10-ounce can whole-cranberry sauce, drained
- ½ cup celery, finely diced
- ¼ cup walnuts, chopped
- 1 cup low-fat sour cream
- Vegetable spray

## MATERIALS

- Large bowl
- Spoon
- Gelatin mold or bowl

## WHAT TO DO

**1** Dissolve gelatin in hot water in large bowl.

**2** Chill until slightly thickened.

**3** Stir cranberry sauce into gelatin until blended.

**4** Stir in celery and nuts.

**5** Fold in sour cream.

**6** Pour into mold sprayed with vegetable spray and chill until set.

**VARIATION:** Substitute flavored Jell-O for gelatin.

**PRACTICAL TIP:** Allow gelatin to thicken a little before adding cranberry sauce, celery, and nuts so that everything will be evenly distributed and doesn't sink to the bottom.

# PILGRIM PIES

Make these individual Pilgrim Pies to serve to each of your guests!

- **Serves:** 6
- **Time:** 20 minutes to prepare
  30 to 35 minutes to bake
- **Complexity:** Easy

## INGREDIENTS

- 2 tablespoons cornstarch
- 1 teaspoon cinnamon
- ¼ teaspoon nutmeg
- 1 cup frozen apple juice concentrate
- 1 tablespoon lemon juice
- 1 tablespoon low-fat margarine
- 6 cups baking apples, sliced, unpeeled
- 6 individual pastry or graham cracker shells

## MATERIALS

- Medium saucepan

## WHAT TO DO

**1** Preheat oven to 350 degrees.

**2** Blend cornstarch, cinnamon, nutmeg, apple juice concentrate, and lemon juice in saucepan.

**3** Cook over medium heat until thickened. Then add margarine.

**4** Put equal number of apple slices into each shell.

**5** Pour apple juice mixture over apples.

**6** Bake at 350 degrees for 30 to 35 minutes, until crust is brown and mixture is sizzling.

**VARIATION:** Make your own mini-pies using your own pastry dough recipe and a muffin tin.

**PRACTICAL TIP:** Cool sauce slightly before pouring over apples.

# TURKEY TREATS

They aren't made from turkey—they just look like turkeys! But look fast—they won't last long!

- **Makes:** 12
- **Time:** 15 minutes to prepare
- **Complexity:** Easy

## INGREDIENTS

- 24 Ritz or other round cracker
- 1 8-ounce package low-fat cream cheese
- 1 package stick pretzels
- 1 box raisins
- 2 slices American cheese, cut into tiny triangles

## MATERIALS

- Knife (for spreading)
- Large platter

## WHAT TO DO

**1** Spread cream cheese on crackers.

**2** Break pretzels in half and stick them around the top half of the cracker to form a fan of feathers.

**3** Top with another cracker spread with cream cheese.

**4** Add two raisins on the upper half of each cracker for eyes, two raisins at the bottom for feet, and a cheese triangle for the beak.

**5** Place turkeys on platter and let your guests gobble them up.

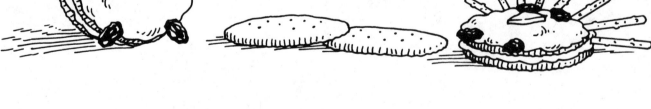

**VARIATIONS:** Use low-fat, low-sugar peanut butter for half the turkeys. Use the round pretzels for a curly fan of tail feathers. Substitute candy corn for cheese.

**PRACTICAL TIPS:** Place broken end of pretzel in toward cracker so it doesn't show when you cover the cracker with a second cracker.

# CHRISTMAS CHEER

Christmas time is party time! And fun foods are an important part of the festivities. Since so many of the holiday foods are creative and fun to make, let the kids help out with designing, cooking, decorating—and, of course, eating—the Christmas cookies, cakes, and candies. You can keep the sugar and fat to a minimum even during the holidays by adapting your recipes, cutting down on not-so-healthy stuff, and substituting nutritious ingredients. Or try some of our Christmas Cheer recipes that present fun foods with healthier alternatives.

# CANDY CANE PARFAIT

Have you ever seen a candy cane in a parfait glass? Your guests will love this how-did-they-do-that dessert!

- **Serves:** 6
- **Time:** 30 minutes to prepare
  2 hours to chill
- **Complexity:** Easy

## INGREDIENTS

- 2 envelopes unflavored gelatin
- 1¼ cups low-fat milk, cold
- ¾ cup orange juice
- 2 eggs
- 4 teaspoons sugar
- 8 ice cubes
- 1 cup frozen strawberries, thawed and drained
- ½ cup low-fat frozen vanilla yogurt

## MATERIALS

- 2 medium bowls
- Medium saucepan
- Spoon
- Blender
- 6 transparent parfait glasses

## WHAT TO DO

1. Combine ½ cup cold milk with gelatin in bowl and let stand 5 minutes.

2. Heat remaining milk in saucepan; don't let the milk boil. Remove from heat.

3. Add gelatin mixture to the heated milk and stir until completely dissolved.

4. Pour into blender and add orange juice, eggs, and sugar. Whirl until blended.

5. Add ice cubes, one at a time, whirling after each addition until ice is melted.

6. Pour 2½ cups of mixture into a bowl.

7. Add strawberries and frozen yogurt to mixture remaining in blender and whirl until blended.

8. In parfait glasses, alternate a layer of orange mixture from the bowl with a layer of pink mixture from the mixer, making 6 layers.

9. Place glasses in refrigerator for 2 hours, until set. Serve.

**VARIATION:** Substitute fresh or frozen cranberries for strawberries.

**PRACTICAL TIP:** Use transparent drinking glasses if you don't have parfait glasses.

# CHOCOLATE NOG

Many kids don't like the taste of eggnog, but add a little chocolate syrup and it becomes magically delicious! Say, what's that ringing noise?

- **Serves:** 12
- **Time:** 10 minutes to prepare
- **Complexity:** Easy

## INGREDIENTS

- 1 quart low-fat eggnog
- 1 5-ounce can low-sugar chocolate syrup
- 1 cup low-fat whipping cream

## MATERIALS

- 12 1-foot lengths of curly red or green ribbon
- 2 small jingle bells
- 12 decorative glasses with stems
- Pair of scissors
- Pitcher or large bowl
- Spoon
- Mixer

## WHAT TO DO

**1** Attach a bell to each ribbon, tie ribbon around glasses, and curl ends of ribbon with scissors.

**2** Combine eggnog and chocolate syrup in a pitcher or large bowl.

**3** Beat whipping cream to form soft peaks.

**4** Fold all but ½ cup of whipping cream into the eggnog mixture.

**5** Pour into glasses and add a spoonful of whipped cream to the top.

**VARIATION:** Heat drink and pour into mugs.

**PRACTICAL TIP:** To make ahead of time, prepare eggnog and chocolate syrup and store in refrigerator, covered, until serving time.

# "GINGERBREAD" MOUSE HOUSE

The kids can make their own "Gingerbread" Mouse Houses, perfect for the Christmas mouse to nibble up!

- **Serves:** 1
- **Time:** 30 minutes to prepare
- **Complexity:** Easy

## INGREDIENTS

- ½ cup low-fat cream cheese frosting (see page 211 for our recipe)
- 6 graham cracker squares
- 10 pretzel sticks
- Small decorative candies, such as red hots, tiny flowers, and sprinkles
- Tube of frosting

## MATERIALS

- Pair of scissors
- 1 8-ounce milk carton, washed and dried
- Knife or spatula

## WHAT TO DO

**1** Cut milk carton in half, vertically, and securely tape the center together to form roof.

**2** Cover 4 sides of carton with cream cheese frosting.

**3** Press 1 graham cracker square on each of the 4 sides to form walls.

**4** Cover top of carton with frosting and attach 2 graham crackers to form roof.

**5** Use pretzels to shape doors and windows, outline walls, and so on. Use frosting from the tube to attach the pretzels.

**6** Decorate house with small candies, attaching them with frosting from the tube.

**VARIATIONS:** Cover the roof with pretzels instead of graham crackers, or cover the whole house with pretzels. Use cookies instead of graham crackers.

**PRACTICAL TIP:** Just provide the materials and let the kids make any kind of Mouse House they choose.

# PEANUT BUTTER REINDEER

Serve these adorable Peanut Butter Reindeer for lunch or at snack time to balance all those candy canes and cookies!

- **Serves:** 4
- **Time:** 15 minutes to prepare
- **Complexity:** Easy

## INGREDIENTS

- 8 slices whole-wheat bread
- ½ cup low-sugar, low-fat peanut butter
- 16 raisins
- 16 twisted pretzels
- 4 maraschino cherries

## MATERIALS

- Knife
- 4 plates

## WHAT TO DO

**1** Spread 4 slices of bread with peanut butter and top each with another slice of bread to make a sandwich.

**2** Cut each sandwich into 4 triangles.

**3** Set 4 triangles on each plate (the 4 triangles will make 4 reindeer, so they should have room between them). One corner of each triangle should point toward the side of the plate facing you.

**4** Stick 2 raisins near the top (wide) side to make eyes.

**5** Place half a cherry at lower corner for nose.

**6** Break twisted pretzels in half to make antler shapes and set antlers at each of the top corners.

**7** Repeat for all triangles and serve.

**VARIATIONS:** Use any kind of filling you like for sandwiches.

**PRACTICAL TIP:** When breaking pretzels, you'll notice they form a slightly twisted fork. Set three-pronged end up.

# STAINED-GLASS COOKIES

The kids can hang these beautiful cookies on the tree, pass them out as gifts, hold them up to a window, or just eat them! But save one for Santa!

- **Makes:** 4 dozen
- **Time:** 30 minutes to prepare
  8 minutes to bake
  5 minutes to cool
- **Complexity:** Easy

## INGREDIENTS

- 2 packages refrigerator sugar cookie dough or you own favorite recipe (or see page 209 for our recipe)
- Flour (for rolling the dough)
- Vegetable spray
- 4 packages of hard candies, such as Life Savers, broken into small pieces

## MATERIALS

- Wax paper
- Rolling pin
- Cookie cutters or glass
- Knife
- Cookie sheet

## WHAT TO DO

**1** Roll cookie dough and roll out on floured surface or wax paper to ⅛-inch thickness.

**2** Cut out holiday-theme cookies with cookie cutters or with a drinking glass.

**3** Preheat oven to 350 degrees.

**4** Cut out a hole in each cookie to fill with candy and place cookies on cookie sheet sprayed with vegetable spray.

**5** Fill holes with candy pieces.

**6** Bake at 350 degrees for 8 minutes, until lightly browned and candy is melted.

**7** Let cool 5 minutes on cookie sheet before removing.

**VARIATION:** Roll the dough into "snakes," shape snakes into designs, and fill open spaces with crushed candy.

**PRACTICAL TIP:** As the candy melts, fill entire space within the cookie with crushed candy so the candy slightly overflows the hole.

# HANUKKAH HUZZAH

Thousands of years ago Maccabees entered the ruined temple and tried to relight the sacred flame. However, the container with the holy oil was smashed and only a small amount of oil remained, enough for only one day. Miraculously, the oil burned for eight days, until more of the holy oil was obtained. Hannukah, known as the Festival of Lights, is the celebration of that miracle.

Families celebrate Hanukkah by lighting candles on the menorah (a special candle holder) every evening and with songs, games, gifts, and, of course, food. Here are some traditional dishes you might want to try, altered slightly to make them more nutritious.

# FROSTED FRUIT

A coating of sweet yogurt makes these grapes and apples a special treat.

- **Serves:** 6
- **Time:** 20 minutes to prepare
- **Complexity:** Easy

## INGREDIENTS

- 1 large bunch of grapes
- 3 apples
- 2 8-ounce containers low-fat fruit yogurt, different flavors

## MATERIALS

- Large platter
- Knife
- 2 small bowls

## WHAT TO DO

**1** Break grapes into small clusters and place in center of platter.

**2** Cut apples into wedges and arrange them around the grapes.

**3** Serve with two bowls of fruit yogurt for dipping.

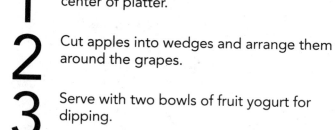

**VARIATIONS:** We've cut down on the amount of sugar this recipe usually includes, so if you prefer, dip the grapes and apples into sugar or honey. Offer other fruits, in addition to the grapes and apples, to dip in yogurt.

**PRACTICAL TIP:** Serve immediately to keep the apples from turning brown.

# LEMON FREEZE

Offer this quick and easy-to-make Lemon Freeze dessert at the end of the meal.

- **Serves:** 8
- **Time:** 10 minutes to prepare
  2 hours to freeze
- **Complexity:** Easy

## INGREDIENTS

- 1 pint heavy whipping cream
- ¼ cup low-fat plain yogurt
- 1 6-ounce can frozen lemonade concentrate
- ½ cup sugar

## MATERIALS

- Blender
- Freezer-safe bowl
- Ice-cream scoop or spoon
- 8 individual dessert dishes

## WHAT TO DO

**1** Combine all ingredients in blender and whirl until thick and smooth, about 2 minutes.

**2** Pour into freezer container and freeze 2 hours or more, until firm.

**3** Scoop into dessert dishes and serve.

**VARIATIONS:** Use other fruit juice concentrates for a variety of flavors.

**PRACTICAL TIP:** Allow to soften about 15 minutes before serving.

# POTATO LATKES

What do you get when you cross a pancake with a hash brown? Make this recipe and you'll see!

- **Serves:** 8
- **Time:** 15 minutes to prepare
  20 minutes to cook
- **Complexity:** Easy

## INGREDIENTS

- 6 medium potatoes, peeled and grated
- 1 medium onion, finely chopped
- 2 eggs
- 2 tablespoons matzo meal
- Vegetable oil
- Applesauce (optional)

## MATERIALS

- Shredder or grater
- Large bowl
- Spoon
- Large electric skillet or frying pan
- Paper towels

## WHAT TO DO

**1** Mix eggs and chopped onion together for several minutes.

**2** Add matzo meal to egg mixture and stir well.

**3** Add grated potatoes and stir well again.

**4** Heat vegetable oil in frying pan over medium heat.

**5** Spoon 1 heaping tablespoon of potato mixture into skillet for each pancake.

**6** Cook 3 to 4 minutes on one side, turn, and cook until golden brown and crispy.

**7** Drain on paper towel. Serve with applesauce.

**VARIATION:** You can use crushed cracker crumbs instead of matzo meal.

**PRACTICAL TIPS:** Serve immediately or keep warm on warming tray until serving time. Leftovers freeze well.

# SESAME-SEED CANDY

**H**oney and sesame seeds were served only on very special occasions in biblical times. Hanukkah is a very special time, so enjoy this delicacy!

- **Makes:** 4 dozen
- **Time:** 30 minutes to prepare
  5 minutes to cool
- **Complexity:** Easy

## INGREDIENTS

- 1 cup honey
- 1 cup sugar
- ½ cup water
- ½ teaspoon cinnamon
- ½ teaspoon ginger
- 1 cup walnuts, chopped
- 2 cups sesame seeds

## MATERIALS

- Heavy saucepan
- Spoon
- Candy thermometer
- Marble slab, board, or platter
- Plastic wrap

## WHAT TO DO

1. Combine honey, sugar, water, and spices in saucepan.

2. Cook over medium heat for about 20 minutes, stirring occasionally, until thermometer reaches 240 degrees (hard-ball stage).

3. Stir in nuts and seeds.

4. Sprinkle water over marble slab and pour candy mixture onto surface.

5. Spread and flatten to ⅛-inch thickness.

6. Cool 5 minutes.

7. When candy is still warm, slice into ½-inch pieces.

8. When candy is cool, wrap individual pieces in plastic wrap.

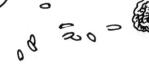

**VARIATION:** Cut large pieces and wrap in colored cellophane as a gift.

**PRACTICAL TIPS:** Candy doesn't harden well on rainy days, so check the weather first. Store leftovers in airtight container

# STAR OF DAVID COOKIES

This cookie recipe is low in cholesterol and fat but sweet enough for the kids to enjoy. And you can create any shape you like with this basic recipe.

- **Makes:** 2 dozen
- **Time:** 20 minutes to prepare
  15 minutes to bake
- **Complexity:** Easy

## INGREDIENTS

- ¾ cup low-fat margarine
- 1 teaspoon vanilla
- 1 teaspoon almond extract
- ½ cup cornstarch
- ½ cup powdered sugar
- 1 cup flour
- Flour (for rolling the dough)
- Vegetable spray
- 1 cup frosting or jam

## MATERIALS

- Large bowl
- Rolling pin
- Knife
- Cookie sheet

## WHAT TO DO

**1** Preheat oven to 325 degrees.

**2** Chop margarine into small bits in large bowl.

**3** Add vanilla, almond extract, cornstarch, sugar, and flour, and mix with hands until dough sticks together and forms a ball.

**4** Roll out dough on floured surface and cut into triangles.

**5** Transfer triangles to cookie sheet sprayed with vegetable spray.

**6** Bake at 325 degrees for 15 minutes, until lightly golden brown around edges.

**7** When cookies are cool, dot center of half the cookies with frosting or jam. Set 1 undotted cookie on top of each dotted cookie, twisting to form 6-pointed stars. Serve.

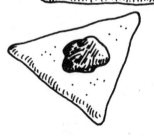

**VARIATION:** Tint dough blue with food coloring.

**PRACTICAL TIP:** Add more flour if dough is sticky.

Appendix
&
Index

# Chocolate Chip Cookies

**Makes:** 4 dozen
**Time:** 15 minutes to prepare
8 to 10 minutes to bake
**Complexity:** Easy

## Ingredients

- ½ cup margarine, softened
- ⅓ cup white sugar
- ⅓ cup brown sugar
- 1 egg
- 1 teaspoon vanilla
- 1 cup flour
- ½ cup oatmeal
- ½ teaspoon baking soda
- ¼ teaspoon salt
- 1 6-ounce package chocolate or carob chips

## Instructions

1 Combine margarine, white and brown sugars, egg, and vanilla. Mix until well blended.

2 Stir in flour, oatmeal, baking soda, and salt. Mix.

3 Add chocolate chips and mix well.

4 Drop by teaspoons onto ungreased cookie sheet.

5 Bake at 375 degrees for 8 to 10 minute, until lightly browned.

6 Remove from oven, cool, and serve.

# Oatmeal Raisin Cookies

**Makes:** 4 dozen
**Time:** 20 minutes to prepare
8 to 10 minutes to bake
**Complexity:** Easy

## Ingredients

- ¾ cup margarine, softened
- ½ cup white sugar
- ¾ cup brown sugar
- 2 eggs
- ⅓ cup milk
- 1½ cups flour
- 1 teaspoon baking soda
- 1 teaspoon baking powder
- ½ teaspoon salt
- 3 cups rolled oats
- 1 cup raisins
- 1 cup chopped nuts (optional)

## Instructions

1 Combine margarine, white and brown sugars, and eggs; beat until fluffy.

2 Stir in milk and blend thoroughly.

3 Add flour, baking soda, baking powder, and salt; mix well.

4 Stir in oats, raisins, and nuts.

5 Drop by tablespoons on cookie sheet sprayed with vegetable spray.

6 Bake at 375 degrees for 8 to 10 minutes, until lightly browned.

7 Remove from oven, cool, and serve.

# Peanut Butter Cookies

**Makes:** 3 dozen
**Time:** 20 minutes to prepare
1 hour to chill
10 to 12 minutes to bake
**Complexity:** Easy

## Ingredients

- ½ cup margarine, softened
- ½ cup low-fat, low-sugar peanut butter
- ½ cup white sugar
- ½ cup brown sugar
- 1 egg
- 1¼ cups flour
- ½ teaspoon baking powder
- ¾ teaspoon baking soda
- ¼ teaspoon salt

## Instructions

1 Combine margarine, peanut butter, white and brown sugars, and egg; mix until well blended.

2 Add flour, baking powder, baking soda, and salt; mix well.

3 Chill dough for 1 hour.

4 Roll dough into 1-inch balls and place 3 inches apart on cookie sheet sprayed with vegetable spray.

5 Flatten with fork in criss-cross manner.

6 Bake at 375 degrees for 10 to 12 minutes, until lightly browned.

7 Remove from oven, cool, and serve.

# Sugar Cookies

**Makes:** 4 dozen
**Time:** 15 minutes to prepare
1 hour to chill
6 to 8 minutes to bake
**Complexity:** Easy

## Ingredients

- ¾ cup margarine, softened
- 1 cup sugar
- 2 eggs
- ½ teaspoon vanilla
- 2½ cups flour
- 1 teaspoon baking powder
- 1 teaspoon salt

## Instructions

1 Combine margarine, sugar, eggs, and vanilla; mix until well blended.

2 Add flour, baking powder, and salt; mix well.

3 Chill dough 1 hour.

4 Roll dough to ⅛-inch thickness on floured board.

5 Cut with cookie cutter and place on ungreased cookie sheet.

6 Bake at 400 degrees for 6 to 8 minutes, until lightly browned.

7 Remove from oven, cool, and serve.

# Gingerbread Cookies

**Makes:** 3 dozen
**Time:** 20 minutes to prepare
1 hour to chill
10 to 12 minutes to bake
**Complexity:** Easy

## Ingredients

- ⅓ cup margarine, softened
- 1 cup brown sugar
- 1½ cups dark molasses
- ⅔ cup cold water
- 7 cups flour
- 2 teaspoons baking soda
- 1 teaspoon salt
- 1 teaspoon allspice
- 1 teaspoon ginger
- 1 teaspoon cloves
- 1 teaspoon cinnamon

## Instructions

1 Combine margarine, sugar, and molasses; mix until well blended.

2 Stir in cold water.

3 Add flour and remaining dry ingredients and mix well.

4 Chill dough for 1 hour.

5 Roll dough to ¼-inch thickness on floured board.

6 Cut out cookies and place on cookie sheet sprayed with vegetable spray, about 1 inch apart.

7 Bake at 350 degrees for 10 to 12 minutes, until lightly browned around edges. Remove from oven, cool, and serve.

# Gingerbread

**Serves:** 12
**Time:** 20 minutes to prepare
35 to 40 minutes to bake
**Complexity:** Easy

## Ingredients

- ½ cup margarine, softened
- ½ cup sugar
- 1 egg
- ½ cup light molasses
- 1½ cups flour
- ¾ teaspoon salt
- ¾ teaspoon baking soda
- ½ teaspoon ginger
- ½ teaspoon cinnamon
- ½ cup boiling water

## Instructions

1 Combine margarine and sugar and beat until light and fluffy.

2 Add egg and molasses and beat thoroughly.

3 Stir in flour, salt, baking soda, ginger, cinnamon, and water; beat well.

4 Pour batter into an 8-by-8-inch pan sprayed with vegetable spray and bake at 350 degrees for 35 to 40 minutes.

5 Remove from oven and cool. Then remove from pan and serve.

# GRAHAM CRACKER CRUST

**Makes:** 1 9-inch pie crust
**Time:** 10 minutes to prepare
6 to 8 minutes to bake or
30 minutes to chill
**Complexity:** Easy

## INGREDIENTS

* 1¼ cups graham cracker crumbs
* 6 tablespoons margarine, melted

## INSTRUCTIONS

1 Combine graham cracker crumbs and melted margarine. Press mixture into bottom and sides of pie pan.

2 Bake at 375 degrees for 6 to 8 minutes, until edges are lightly browned. OR Chill unbaked for 30 minutes.

# CHOCOLATE WAFER CRUST

**Makes:** 1 9-inch pie crust
**Time:** 10 minutes to prepare
30 or more minutes
to chill
**Complexity:** Easy

## INGREDIENTS

* 1½ cups chocolate wafer cookie crumbs
* 6 tablespoons margarine, melted

## INSTRUCTIONS

1 Combine crumbs with melted margarine and mix well. Press mixture into bottom and sides of pie pan.

2 Chill to set.

# CREAM CHEESE FROSTING

**Makes:** 2 cups
**Time:** 10 minutes
**Complexity:** Easy

## INGREDIENTS

* 2 8-ounce packages low-fat cream cheese, softened
* ½ cup powdered sugar

## INSTRUCTIONS

1 Combine cream cheese and sugar and mix well.

**TIP:** The above recipe is equal to 2 cans low-fat cream cheese frosting. If you need more or less frosting, adjust the recipe accordingly.

# Index

# Index

# Index

# Index

# Order Form

| Qty. | Title | Author | Order No. | Unit Cost | Total |
|------|-------|--------|-----------|-----------|-------|
| | Bad Case of the Giggles | Lansky, B. | 2411 | $15.00 | |
| | Best Baby Name Book | Lansky, B. | 1029 | $5.00 | |
| | Best Baby Shower Book | Cooke, C. | 1239 | $7.00 | |
| | Best Bridal Shower Game Book | Cooke, C. | 6060 | $3.95 | |
| | Best Couple's Shower Game Book | Cooke, C. | 6061 | $3.95 | |
| | Best Party Book | Warner, P. | 6089 | $8.00 | |
| | Best Wedding Shower Book | Cooke, C. | 6059 | $7.00 | |
| | Dads Say the Dumbest Things! | Lansky/Jones | 4220 | $6.00 | |
| | Familiarity Breeds Children | Lansky, B. | 4015 | $7.00 | |
| | Free Stuff for Kids | Free Stuff Editors | 2190 | $5.00 | |
| | Grandma Knows Best | McBride, M. | 4009 | $6.00 | |
| | If We'd Wanted Quiet/Poems for Parents | Lansky, B. | 3505 | $12.00 | |
| | Kids' Holiday Fun | Warner, P. | 6000 | $12.00 | |
| | Kids' Party Cookbook | Warner, P. | 2435 | $12.00 | |
| | Kids' Party Games and Activities | Warner, P. | 6095 | $12.00 | |
| | Kids Pick the Funniest Poems | Lansky, B. | 2410 | $15.00 | |
| | Moms Say the Funniest Things! | Lansky, B. | 4280 | $6.00 | |
| | Mother Murphy's Law | Lansky, B. | 1149 | $5.00 | |
| | Poetry Party | Lansky, B. | 2430 | $12.00 | |
| | | | | Subtotal | |
| | | | Shipping and Handling (see below) | | |
| | | | MN residents add 6.5% sales tax | | |
| | | | | **Total** | |

YES! Please send me the books indicated above. Add $2.00 shipping and handling for the first book and 50¢ for each additional book. Add $2.50 to total for books shipped to Canada. Overseas postage will be billed. Allow up to four weeks for delivery. Send check or money order payable to Meadowbrook Press. No cash or COD's, please. Prices subject to change without notice. **Quantity discounts available upon request.**

**Send book(s) to:**

Name _____ Address _____

City _____ State _____ Zip _____

Telephone (_____)_____ P.O. number (if necessary) _____

Payment via:

❑ Check or money order payable to Meadowbrook Press (No cash or COD's, please)    Amount enclosed $ _____

❑ Visa (for orders over $10.00 only)  ❑ MasterCard (for orders over $10.00 only)

Account # _____ Signature _____ Exp. Date _____

**A *FREE* Meadowbrook Press catalog is available upon request.**
You can also phone us for orders of $10.00 or more at 1-800-338-2232.

**Mail to:**                           **Meadowbrook, Inc.**
                          18318 Minnetonka Boulevard, Deephaven, MN 55391
Phone (612) 473-5400             Toll-Free 1-800-338-2232                    Fax (612) 475-0736